The Chiltern Line

of the Great Western and Great Central Railways

Bill Simpson

Published by Lamplight Publications
260 Colwell Drive
Witney
Oxfordshire

First Published 2015

Copyright Bill Simpson and Lamplight Publications

All rights reserved

No part of this publication may be reproduced,
stored in a retrieval system or transmitted in
any form or by any means electronic,
mechanical, photocopying, recording or otherwise
without the prior approval of the publisher

ISBN: 978 1 899246 59 5

Printed and bound at Berforts Information Press
Southfield Road, Eynsham, Oxford OX29 4JB

Tunnels under Lords' cricket ground succeeding against very stern opposition!

Contents

	Introduction	5
Chapter 1.	Another Way	8
Chapter 2.	A Parallel Aim - The Great Western Railway	16
Chapter 3.	New Lights from Old Lamps	23
Chapter 4.	Resisting the Tide of Closure	29
Chapter 5.	Stations Along the Line	35
Chapter 6.	Beyond the New Horizon	153
	Further Reading and Index	158

Acknowledgements

The Author would like to express his gratitude to the following: the staff of the Brent Museum and Archive. Buckinghamshire Collection at the Buckinghamshire Record Office, Roger Carpenter, Michael Dewy (Bucks Free Press) Phil Grant (Wembley History Society), Chris Green (Network SouthEast), Catherine Grigg (High Wycombe Museum), Jackie H Kay (High Wycombe History Society), Gaby Higgs (St Marylebone Society), Rob Riley, the staff at the Oxford Archives, , Peter Tozer (High Wycombe History Society) Wembley History Society, Also to all of the photographers that have so generously allowed me to use their photographs.

Marylebone station on June 10, 1966 with Black Five no 44920 waiting with the Nottingham 2.38 pm train. By this time the steam locomotives were working out their last few years and became very neglected calling on a great deal from the crews that were rostered to keep time with them.

R M Casserley

A bridge surviving in use for the fertilizer trains over the road between the villages of Quainton and Edgcott, it remained as a structure until 2013. It was then removed and replaced with a concrete structure supporting a roadway suitable to withstand the weight of large lorries going to the new incinerator plant being built at Grendon Underwood.

Bill Simpson

Introduction

A great deal has already been written about the GWR&GCR Joint Committee lines and certain facts are established. The intention of this book is not to simply repeat them but to add, where possible, with new photographs and data. With the passage of time the process of change is bound to be realised and the remarkable experience of this system is that it came so close to the brink of extinction and fought back, not only to survive, but to prosper. It is not an experience normally associated with railways in the United Kingdom over the past sixty or seventy years.

For some forty years I have lived close to the railway and used it very often, so I was startled to realise that a closure notice had been posted on Marylebone station platform in 1984. The closure of a London terminus is thankfully not too common an event.

In February 1981 I had the good fortune to be invited to join Oxford University Railway Society on a rail tour over Oxon & Bucks lines. Although we got off from Oxford in a foggy start it cleared to bright sunshine eventually and the day was enjoyed, but tarnished with the sense that the

THE CHILTERN LINE

railways seemed to have a bleak future and the visits at various points felt like a *homage* to former glories. The faded gleam that had been the Great Central Railway with their proud 'Atlantics' and 'Directors' hauling dining car trains. The mighty GWR 'King' class hammering through the Chilterns with two-hour expresses to Birmingham contrasted with this bleak twilight.

Subsequently however, some thirty years later the situation has become optimistic in a way that would have seemed impossible then. The addition of track to return to double after being singled between Princes Risborough and Aynho Junction promised a new direction for railway services. The formation and launching of Network SouthEast on June 1986 and the continuing progress with Chiltern Railway's Evergreen 3 project creating a new Oxford - London link. Also the proposed re-opening of the Oxford to Cambridge service with East - West Rail. The project for a new main line - HS2 has raised intense conflict and controversy on a scale concerning railways not seen for many years. The imposition of this has paralleled in history that of George Stephenson's suggested route very similar to this in the 1830s for a proposed London & Birmingham Railway. This also was hotly opposed!

We now live in an age of railways operated by competing regional franchises and the Chiltern Railways franchise, which serves Aylesbury and the former GWR line to Birmingham has probably become the greatest success story in this railway operating system. It fulfils the remit of providing fast, comfortable and regular trains. Indeed the line to Birmingham has now such an intensive service that it must surely rival the period of the Great Western Railway!

The prospect of that service being extended to include Oxford is an exciting opportunity. A new station being built at Water Eaton north of Oxford will obviate many travellers from going into the city at all, which must be an advantage to the hard-pressed Oxford station, relieving to some extent the narrow roads of the city.

This will bring a concentration of services into the London terminus of Marylebone, a high contrast to its closure.

There is a historic irony in this. As the Manchester Sheffield & Lincolnshire Railway's independent terminus to their London extension it was very much opposed. And when it was at last built it was not the success that had been optimistically anticipated. Nevertheless with their new name - Great Central Railway, it did operate some magnificent trains and provided essential traffic routes during two world wars.

The following pages present a visual description of the lines of the Great Western & Great Central Joint Committee through the trials of the

INTRODUCTION

grouping in 1923 and the sad hopelessness following nationalisation in 1948. Bringing the story, as far as is possible, to the present. There is now a new optimism for rail travel as passengers find other things to occupy themselves with during a journey, preferring to avoid the frustrations of traffic jams and the intense concentration needed these days when driving a car. There is now much to look forward to for rail travellers, at last.

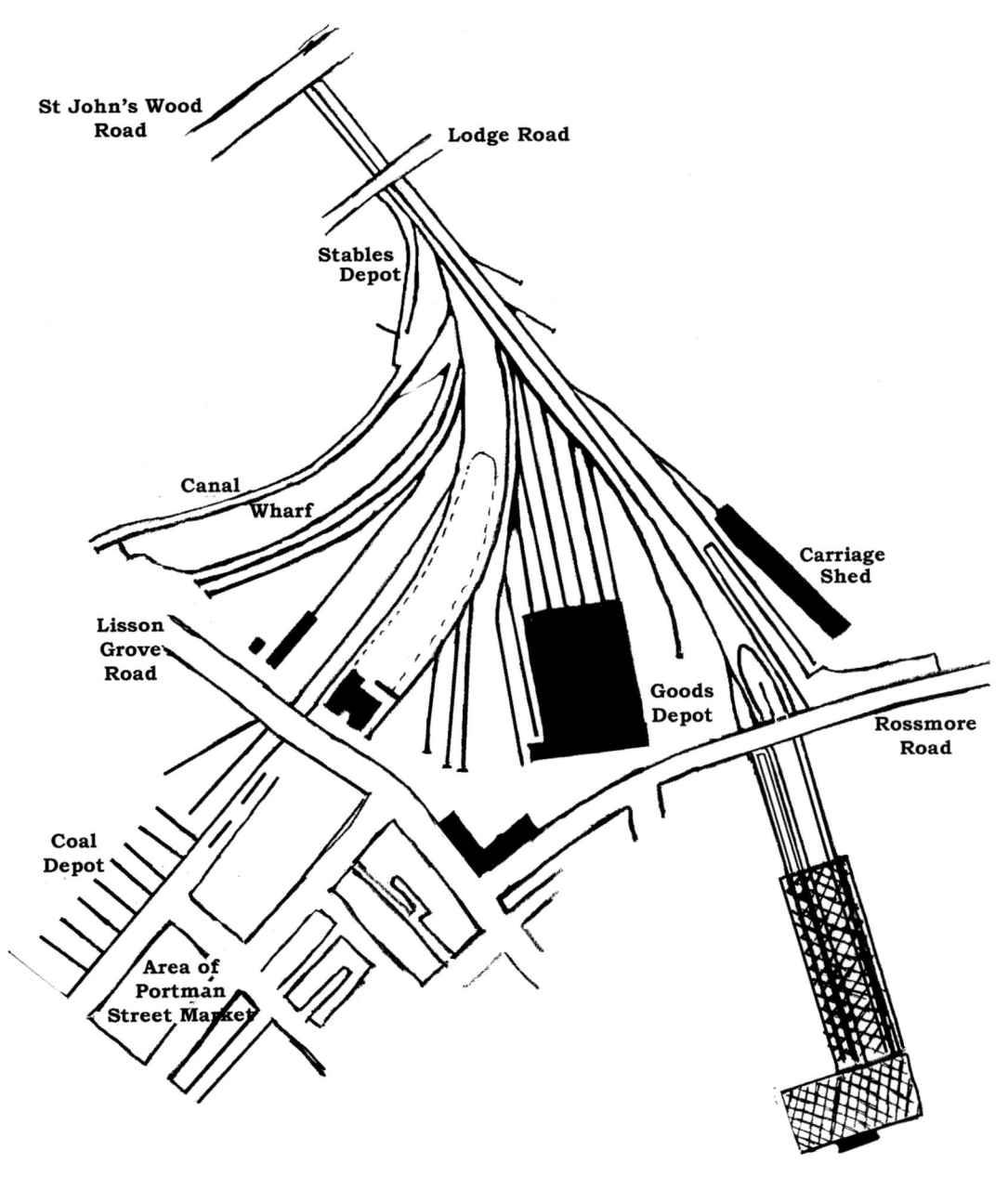

A general ground plan view of Marylebone at its most complete.

Bill Simpson

In the Spring of 1949 N5 0-6-2T LNER 9369 is engaged in carriage shunting at Marylebone.
Neil Sprinks

Another Way

The Manchester, Sheffield & Lincolnshire Railway is often a subject seen from that perfect viewpoint - hindsight. In its ambitions to reach London many would say that it came too late to the table with its London Extension and in so doing overreached itself financially.

Competing railways had already filled in the spaces between ridges of rising ground north of London. The London & Birmingham Railway in 1838, the Great Northern Railway in 1850, the Midland Railway that finally made its statement of epic grandeur with the opening of St Pancras and its grand hotel in 1868. The Metropolitan Railway more modestly came north in 1868 utilising the St John's Wood Railway. The Great Western Railway had been more fortunate by building its line to some extent along the alluvial ridge of the River Thames 1838-41.

The Manchester, Sheffield & Lincolnshire Railway was a company, as its name describes, that was strung across the Pennine reaches of the north of England between those cities including Grimsby in Lincolnshire. A former secretary of the Buckinghamshire Railway, Edward Watkin, became general manger of that company and then the chairman in 1864. He proved to be fired with as much industrious ambition as many other leaders in the Victorian period and wanted the company to have a connection with the capital to exploit contracts from the Yorkshire coalfields.

At first he courted the Great Northern Railway for shared access on their metals to Kings Cross but was not successful. The Midland Railway were also approached but were similarly unaccommodating.

This left the frustrated Watkin and his directors with their boardroom deliberations of building their own line. It was now the 1860s and the outer districts of London had moved on rapidly since 1838 expanding across open fields and rapidly building up over the area of any prospective terminus and its access. Although, as it became evident later, much of the displacement for the terminus involved demolition of impoverished housing settlements in a rather unsavory area.

Further, the survey would have to include the centres of Nottingham, Leicester and Rugby, which meant competing with the other companies. The only town of any size to appreciate the arrival of the new railway would be Lutterworth. Time was not on Watkin's side.

An opportunity came in the expansion of the erstwhile new underground railway, the Metropolitan Railway, building a new line north; it opened a service to Swiss Cottage in 1863. And was therefore completed as far as its aim, using the tiny St John's Wood Railway which opened on April 13, 1868. This became the first probe north from the yet, uncompleted Circle Line. Watkin's mind must have sparkled with an idea of what he might achieve if this railway operated by the Metropolitan Railway could be persuaded to move north and join with a south extension of the MS&LR.

Watkin was adept at positioning himself ideally on the railway management chessboard of the time. He became chairman of the Metropolitan Railway on August 7, 1872 and he used his position with consummate dexterity. Although the Circle Line was as yet incomplete, as the matters with the Metropolitan & District Railway to move in co-existent partnership were not resolved until 1884. And the Metropolitan had extended itself financially also, as railway companies nearly always did.

Nevertheless, Watkin convinced the board of the Metropolitan that an opportunity to purchase what we would now term as 'green field' sites on each side of an extension north would reap benefits for the Metropolitan with domestic settlements of a London work force in the suburbs. For this enterprise the Metropolitan Estates Committee was established. Further, that essential new line would give a connection to the M&SLR extension with a route through the Chiltern ridge to reach the capital. A hinted exposition to the board to avail itself of Baker Street terminus was a proposal too far, even for Watkin, who could not employ his persuasive skills successfully on that particular proposition. Looking at Baker Street now one can easily comprehend that this would have been impossible.

With seemingly inexhaustible energy he became the chairman of the South Eastern Railway in 1866 and pronounced, at some stage, the prospect of a main line from the north to Paris through a new Channel Tunnel. Confusion has followed ever since on the sincerity of this proclamation. Given the considerable challenges to the technology of a hundred years later and enormous financial resources to realise this achievement it suggests a potential folly greater even than his failed tower project at Wembley. The subject is excellently detailed in a paper by Grahame Boyes in the *Journal of the Railway & Canal Historical Society Special 200th Edition, Volume 35 Part 10,* December 2007 with the title *The Origins of a Modern Myth.* Mr Boyes explains copiously how assertions can be turned into 'facts' over a period of time. One would deduce not before time!

So it was that a new terminus would have to be built and the line would have to divert from the Metropolitan at Canfield Place. Thence beneath north London in a series of tunnels until reaching the space created near Portman Market in the district of Marylebone.

The First survey for the MS&LR London Extension was placed before parliament in April 1891. However, some differences with the GNR at Annesley had to be reconciled so the Bill was presented again, but was forestalled by a dissolution of parliament. It was submitted again and finally passed on March 28, 1893, which included the new terminus at Marylebone. Due to financial difficulties little was done before 1894. The Act included powers to subscribe by Watkin's other companies, the South Eastern Railway and the Metropolitan Railway. By a further Act of August 1, 1897 it changed its name to the Great Central Railway.

It was built across 93 miles from Annesley Junction in Nottinghamshire to Quainton Road station in Buckinghamshire where it joined with the Metropolitan Railway. Including stations at Nottingham, Rugby and Leicester and of course Lutterworth. Unlike the green fields, wooded enclosures and small towns in the countryside that faced the first railways the Great Central had to demolish streets of housing in large cities along the route which must have been at horrendous cost. Also the line from the Metropolitan at Canfield Place to the new terminus at Marylebone faced the girded opposition of Marylebone Cricket Club.

Referring once more to the excellent Grahame Boyes article, he includes also the distortion following on from the

ANOTHER WAY

There could have been few occasions for the workforce to pause for photographs as the work was undertaken at considerable pace. Here is a good view of one of the number of 'steam navvy' machines. Although somewhat cumbersome by modern standards they served an essential role in earth moving with greater speed. This view is to the north of Bicester.

Barry Davis Collection

Channel Tunnel myth that the GCR extension was built to continental loading gauge, the Berne Conference Gauge. The published gauge of the MS&L line was in fact less than this gauge, which was not, itself established until 1913! Where it did triumph was in the gain from most of its heavy engineering work with a ruling gradient of 1 in 176 and no curve of less than one mile radius. A remarkable factor is that the GCR line was the most economically adaptable line for a channel tunnel to the north as it would have cost less to modify it than say the Midland or the ex-LNWR line.

Construction began in November 1894 when the people of Middlesex, Hertfordshire, Buckinghamshire, Northamptonshire, Leicestershire and Nottinghamshire must have felt that the days of the 'estates' of shanty towns housing gangs of rough mud coloured men wielding picks and shovels and clogging country lanes with heavy horse teams were behind them. Many did not take kindly to its repetition.

Nevertheless the new line was a thing of engineering beauty with its super elevated track on gentle curves and only one level crossing. A tunnel was dug of 1 mile 1237 yards long at

THE CHILTERN LINE

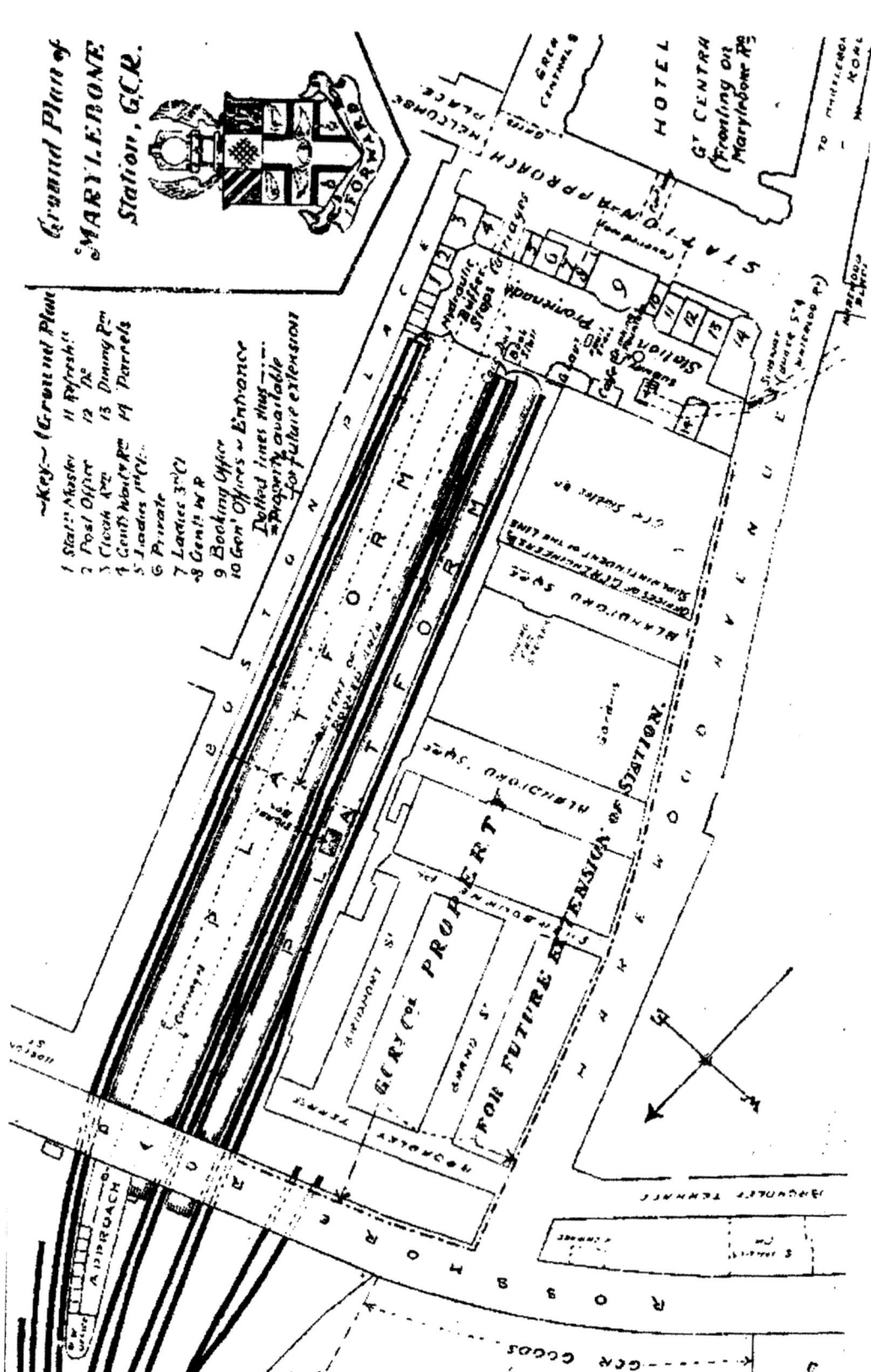

A ground plan view of Marylebone station published by the GCR showing the streets alongside purchased by the railway company and provided to extend the station which was never realised.

Great Central Railway

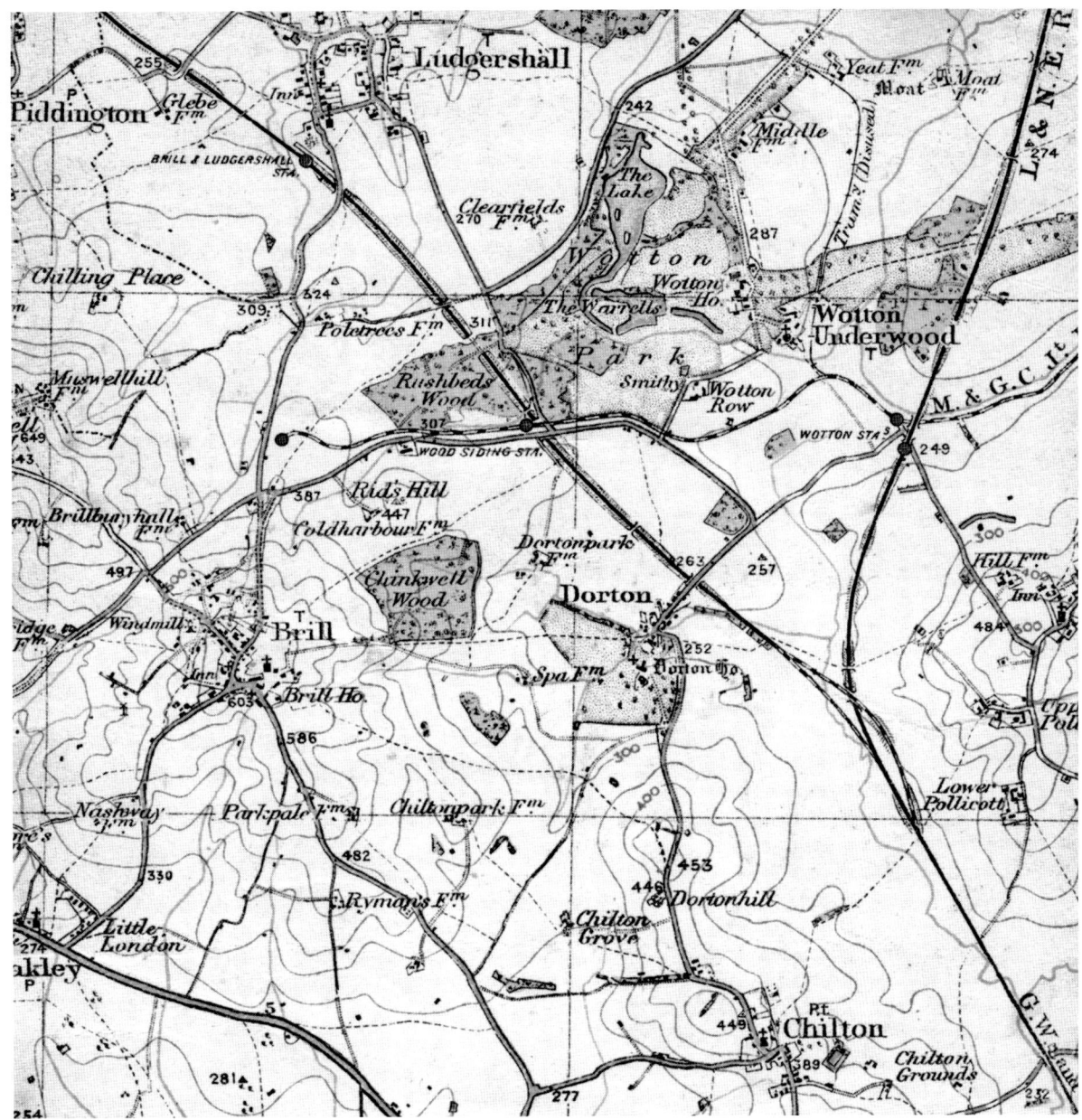

The junction connection at Ashendon, the broken line section denoting single track. Note the Brill branch line passing beneath at Wotton with its own thin line mineral branch to Kingswood (1914).
Ordnance Survey

Catesby. Building the line for high speed running was very much aided by the use of the 'steam navvies', cumbersome machines that gouged out the earth with what would have taken hundreds of shovels full. A large number of these machine were backed up by the ubiquitous Manning Wardle 0-6-0ST engines that seemed to be everywhere portrayed in the book by L T C Rolt *Making of A Railway* (1971).

Stations utilised the over bridges beneath which they constructed long island platforms which emphasised a more modern look and allowed other lines to be laid alongside if needed.

THE CHILTERN LINE

The gated entrance arch to Marylebone station that was originally intended for horse drawn vehicles but now serves as the main entrance.

Bill Simpson

These were built on this design even in the midst of large rural areas which probably supplied more milk and coal traffic than passengers.

The line opened for coal traffic on August 1897 reaching London on July 25, 1898. A special first passenger train ran on March 9, 1899, for the public on March 15. Sir Edward Watkin saw the opening but had had to retire before construction; he died in 1901. He saw its triumph, but not its demise in terms of problems that followed.

It did however supply another important outlet for the coalfields of south Yorkshire, Derbyshire and Nottinghamshire for which it competed for this traffic with the GNR and Midland who were inclined to take the view that it had divided the cake too many ways as the GCR was not a success at their own level. Nevertheless the GCR carried ore from Consett to South Wales, fish from Grimsby and Hull and bananas from Bristol, it may have struggled to take form but when it did it was imposing and competitive. Significantly the new connections that followed cross-country north - south proved an essential advantage, particularly between Culworth Junction and Banbury North, which saw very heavy traffic.

By 1905 twelve daytime expresses left Marylebone for Leicester, Nottingham and Sheffield. Five continued to Manchester via the notorious Woodhead Tunnel.

Two carried on to Bradford Exchange. Bradshaw's had now a significant new railway to add to their guide and timetables.

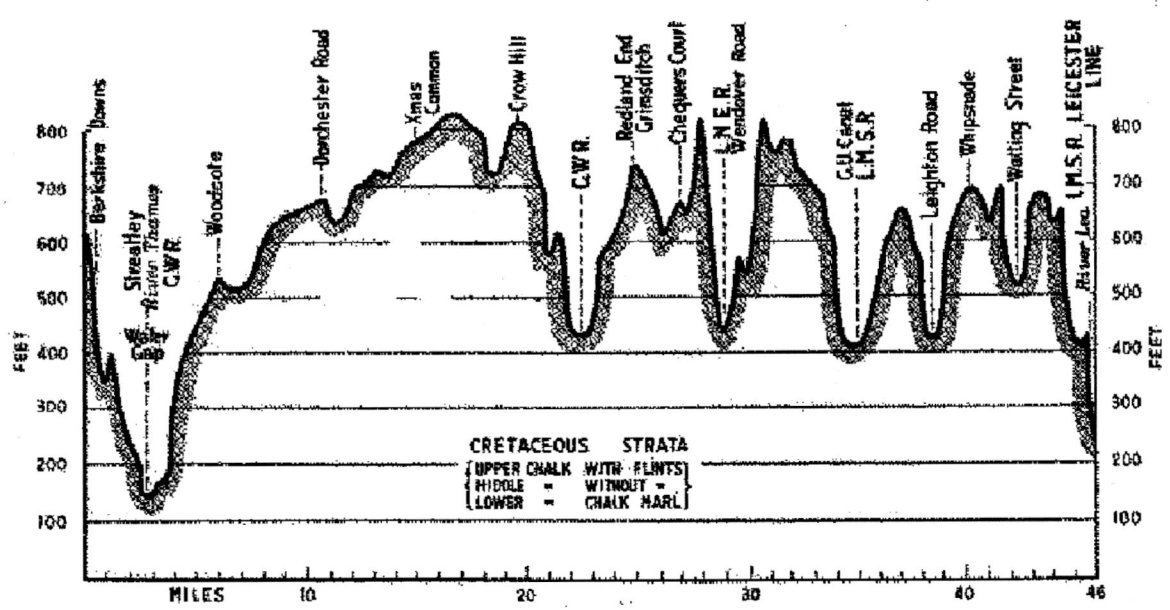

A compressed view of the limited gaps in the Chiltern ridge of hills which presented a major obstacle to railway building north of London.

Author's Collection

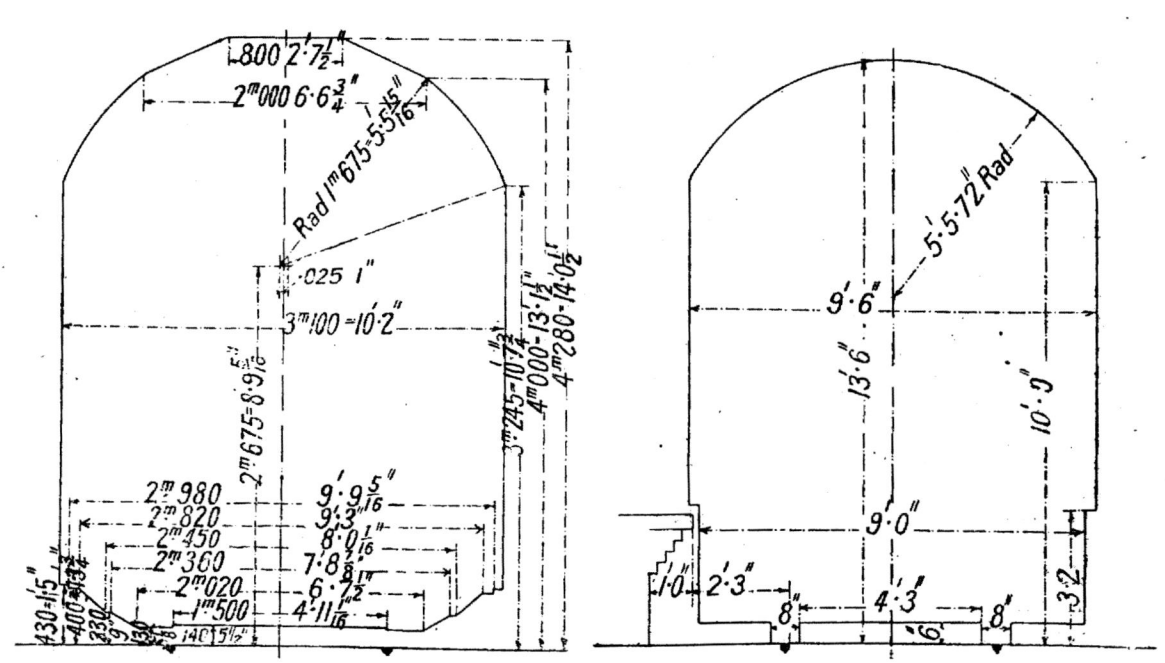

1. Berne Conference Gauge.　　　　2. Proposed Standard Gauge for Great Britain.

Aynho Park station in the early 1960s with an 'up' train headed by a 'Castle' class watched by a person in the relaxation of summer sunshine as it imperviously rushes through.

Andrew Bratton

A Parallel Aim
The Great Western Railway

The Wycombe Railway, after some early failed proposals, succeeded with an Act of June 1852 to build a branch from the GWR's broad gauge main line leaving at Maidenhead to the town of High Wycombe. This was the most significant town in the district that had not as yet been reached by railway and had an industry of furniture making. The new railway was opened on August 1, 1854. A number of conflicting proposals by other companies spurred the GWR on to support an extension of this railway to Princes Risborough and Thame with a further Act of August 1857. This sparse region of scattered villages and small towns became rapidly connected with new railways as another Act of June 28, 1861 was to extend the railway from Princes Risborough to Aylesbury. A town that hitherto had been a railway preserve of the LNWR with their branch from Cheddington (1839).

The line to Thame was opened on August 1, 1862 and to Aylesbury on October 1, 1863. By October 24, 1864 the Thame line was extended further to Kennington Junction on the Didcot - Oxford - Birmingham line. This gave the GWR an alternative to Oxford when the line via Reading and Didcot had works problems and was often used as a by-pass route.

This system was eventually to prove fortuitous for the GWR who absorbed it from its original local company origins and operated the lines from 1867. By 1871 all of it was altered from the original broad gauge to standard gauge with another branch line being added at Princes Risborough to Chinnor and Watlington in 1872.

This preamble is an illustration of the history of the lines that the GWR were able to take advantage of when they found a need to shorten their route to Birmingham. There had long been a need for the company to have an alternative route from the line via Reading, Didcot and Oxford to Birmingham. Importantly the cost of a new line may be underwritten by the developing Birkenhead-American boat traffic that wanted a fast direct line to London. There could not have been a more perfect motivation of mutual need than the coincidence between the GCR and GWR. The new line when complete would give the GWR a route nineteen miles shorter than the route via Oxford and two miles shorter than that of the LNWR from Euston.

It had not taken long for problems to develop in the arrangements between the interests of the Metropolitan & GCR Joint Committee with the former working of fast suburban services with regular stops against those of the GCR with north country expresses that wanted to continue at a pace to and from the city. Also the development of coal and freight at Marylebone. Speed over the Met lines was reduced to 45 mph, with 25 mph at Rickmansworth. So under the distinctive management leadership of Sir Sam Fay, a strong character, the GCR found its alternative.

The Act for the GWR&GCR Joint Committee came into force on August 1, 1899. The survey was for a line from Neasden where the GCR could depart from the Metropolitan lines to Northolt where it would join the GWR scheme for nearly 34 miles to a location north of Princes Risborough near the village of Ashendon. Here a new connecting line would be put in to allow the GCR to rejoin their main line at Grendon Underwood. This would be 5 miles longer than the Met route but would allow the trains to run at 70 mph over the new lines. The new Committee was composed of an equal number of GCR and GWR directors.

An essential link to the workings of the GWR to and from Paddington was

THE CHILTERN LINE

An early map showing the route of the Wycombe Railway in 1862 which includes the branch to Thame. Note the broken line indicating the erstwhile planned route of the Aylesbury & Buckingham Railway to Steeple Claydon.

Author's Collection

the Acton & Wycombe Railway (GWR) August 6, 1897 which connected with a line from Old Oak Common to the former Wycombe Railway branch.

The line from Northolt Junction to High Wycombe came under the Joint Committee, the section beyond High Wycombe to Princes Risborough was sold to the Joint Committee for £225,000. That was before lines of improvement were added.

The Joint Committee also authorised fifteen miles of railway from Princes Risborough to rejoin the exclusive GCR line at Grendon Underwood.

It was later decided by both companies that the line from the new junction near the village of Ashendon to Grendon Underwood (5¾ miles) would be exclusively the GCR responsibilities so it was transferred to GCR ownership on November 20, 1905.

The Northolt to High Wycombe contract was let at £580,000 to R W Pauling & Co, Westminster.

Mackay & Davies of Cardiff won the High Wycombe to Princes Risborough contract at £116,797. Messrs Nott & Sons built the Haddenham to Grendon Underwood section for £170,276. Webster & Cannon added two stations in 1904 for £1,514. All was under the auspices of the GWR resident engineer G H Mackillop.

All of the works began in June 1902. To Paulings would fall the reconstruction of the single line viaduct at High Wycombe, station and goods yard, which would have four tracks. West Wycombe station would have to be entirely rebuilt.

Once beyond High Wycombe the line had to modify the shortcomings of the original branch. With a new line doubling the route including a short tunnel constructed at Saunderton, the original line of 1 in 88 was eased somewhat and became the 'down' road. A new 'up' line with the easier gradient of 1 in 167 was built in a cutting. The station at Princes Risborough had to be totally rebuilt.

The Northolt Junction to Grendon Underwood opened for goods traffic on November 20, 1905. Passenger Traffic was introduced on April 2, 1906. The GCR wasted little time in taking advantage of this free running opportunity as on July 2, 1906 they diverted three of their Marylebone - Manchester and Manchester - Marylebone trains over the new lines.

The track beyond Princes Risborough had a very restricted curvature. Thus was created the Aynho & Ashendon Railway authorised under the GWR Railways Act of July 11, 1905. This, in keeping with the grand design, had also to be built to allow fast running, which was the whole point for the GWR. It was laid out by Walter Armstrong the GWR works engineer with a ruling gradient of 1 in 193 and had curves of not less than two miles

THE CHILTERN LINE

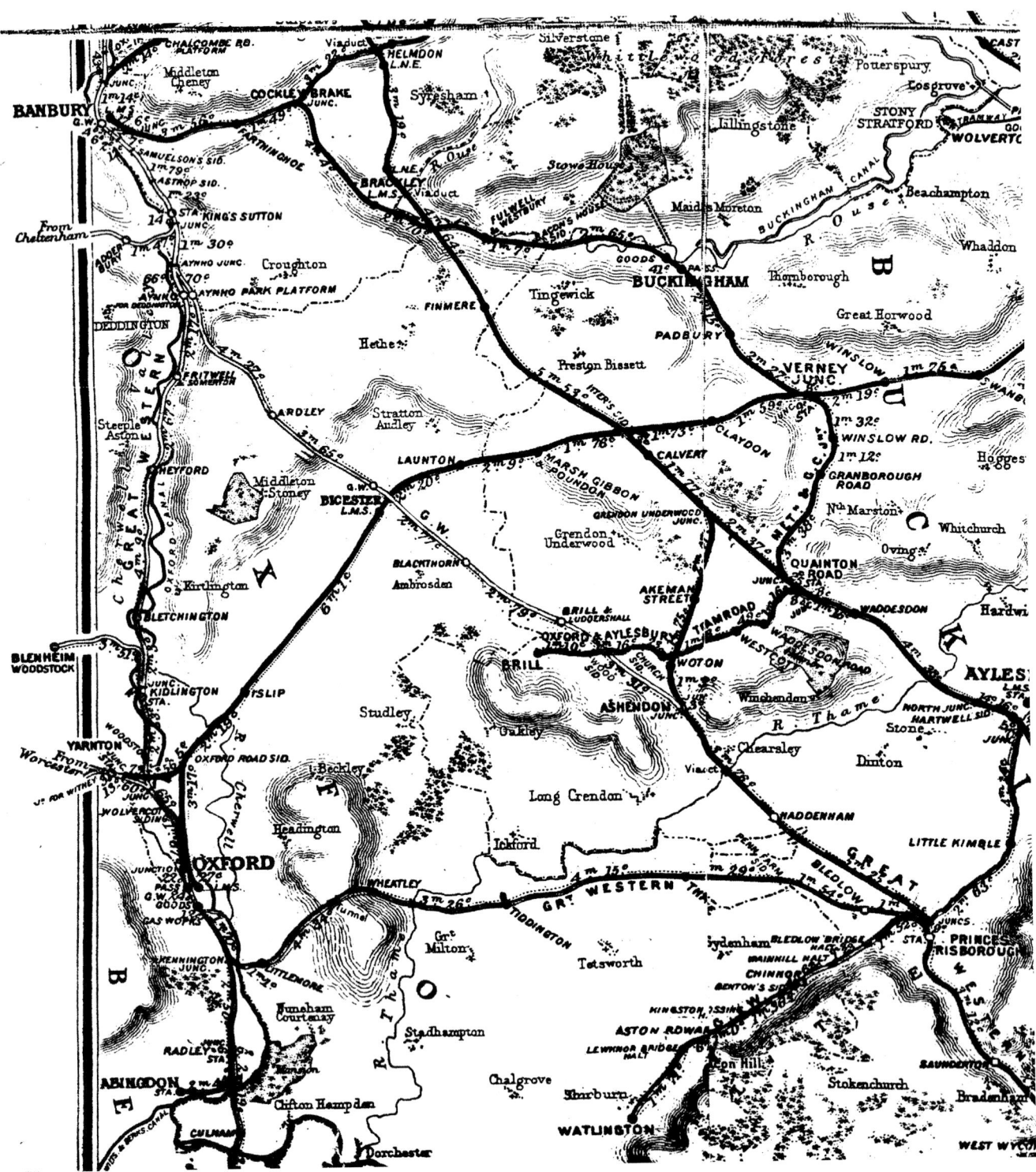

The route of the line of the GWR from Princes Risborough to Banbury including the GCR route to Helmdon in the 1930s.

Authors Collection

A PARALLEL AIM

radius. This proved to be quite an undertaking for the GWR and Scott & Middleton did not start work on it until the Joint Committee part of the railway had been fully opened on April 2, 1906. The contract required movement of three million cubic yards of earth and rock, which, in the manner of such things, is done to establish equable alignment of cuttings with embankments. The route also needed fifty bridges.

The design of these stations marks out the embodiment of station design in the twentieth century, minimal elaboration in brick with some stone lintels and dressings, the key aim being mainly functional and they retain a very sturdy appearance to the present day. Spacious cantilevered roofs supported on steel framework leave the platforms clear of obstruction except where ex-tended canopies have been installed.

Alongside the main line loops were built to hold eighty wagon trains. The GWR were obviously applying a great deal of resource borne of experience.

The line opened for business on April 4, 1910, for the testing period of running goods trains. Passengers were allowed to book from July 1.

A Timetable for the Wycombe Railway published in the *Oxford Times* in 1862.

THE CHILTERN LINE

A much begrimed 9F no 92069 on the 'up' line at the Saunderton separate track levels. The date is October 1, 1964 a time when many steam locomotives looked in a very sad state.

J F Aylard/Initial Photographics

The lines divide with the train going south on the newly built 'up' line. The other line being the original modified line that became the 'down'.

Bill Simpson

New Lights from Old Lamps

The Great Central enjoyed merely fourteen years as a single enterprise company, in that time it had done a great deal which contributed to the needs of the country. It made an outstanding impression with its dining car expresses hauled by beautifully well-balanced looking engines like the Robinson 4-4-2 'Atlantics' and 4-4-0 'Directors'. They had built and opened Immingham Docks that brought a knighthood for Sam Fay.

As the Manchester, Sheffield & Lincolnshire Railway it had paid a 3% dividend, as the GCR it never paid any at all on ordinary shares. It spent the colossal sum of £2,262,622 on docks. They supported and leased the extensive development at Immingham. But did show enterprising innovation by setting up its own publicity department in 1902. Some towns like Mansfield gratefully received better services than hitherto by the arrival of the GCR.

At the outbreak of hostilities in 1914 its service was combined with all the railways to serve the national need. The new system of GWR and GCR Joint Committee lines were pressed into heavy service with large freight yards at Woodford Halse, Banbury and in London, which were utilised to the full extent.

During the War the administration of the railways came under the Railway Executive Committee, which had to assimilate the use of the differing companies to be co-ordinated to a direct single purpose during the emergency. The innocent queues of laughing and joking young men enrolling in Kitchener's Army was morosely dispelled by the subsequent reality. This became true in so many ways. The nation that emerged from that war in 1918 did so to a changed world. The loss of innocence was reflected in society at large which became embittered that it had not only experienced a brutal war, but had not realised the better and fairer society that had been promised from the sacrifice. The pre-war stability loginand social order was not to be seen again.

The railways had done their bit but could not go back to their former shape. Road competition was a burgeoning threat as former dusty pathways became built up tarmacadam roads for thousands of ex WD vehicles and their drivers looking to find employment for their new skills as bus drivers, carrier wagon drivers or any other motor vehicles contrivance that could be engineered in the new automobile age.

Under the Railways Act of 1921 compensation settlements were administered to post war claims by the companies. Significantly the GWR & GCR were in receipt of an amount of £33,403 which may have seemed much by early twentieth century values but must have been a mere token in terms of the extra train working and wear and tear on the infrastructure.

The railways re-formed into what came to be known as 'The Big Four', four new stock holding companies, the GWR, LMS. LNER and the Southern Railway. The Joint Committee role was complicated by the fact the GWR remained largely unchanged but the former GCR was merged into the new LNER.

Much has been written in books and articles covering the years of these four companies and for details these are easily available. It was a dovetailing of former resolute competitors, the LNWR and the Midland Railway, The Great Northern Railway and the Great Central Railway, the former smarting somewhat by the incursion on its territories by the latter. However, Kings Cross and Marylebone did work together. There is some irony in this insomuch as the GNR, GCR, and GER had attempted to combine in 1909 but were forbidden to do so as a gross monopoly.

The poet W H Auden described the thirties as 'that low dishonest decade', following the world crash of 1929 which brought the misery of mass unemployment and deprivation to millions followed by an industrial slump that became the harbinger to the gathering threat of World War II which was declared in 1939. The expanded freight facilities utilised in World War 1 would be called upon again to

A Robinson locomotive no 6071 of the former GCR in LNER days with a train of GWR coaches at Banbury GWR in the 1930s. A train no doubt bound to pass over the junction north of Banbury that would take it on over what had by now become the LNER route to the northern cities. Note the Motor Coach in the bay alongside. The station is largely in its original form that was to change after the second World War. Something of a priority in the British Railways Modernisation Plan of 1955 with a new goods shed built in brick, and an entire rebuild of the station buildings in 1958.

C R L Coles

provide essential support, particularly the section between Banbury and Culworth Junction with extended goods yards built at both ends. The GWR had been able to gain from the government's funding under the Loans and Guarantees Act of 1929 intended to relieve unemployment by building the freight yard at Banbury to a 'hump' marshalling yard with much greater speed and capacity. This opened on May 15, 1931.

Once again the section of only a few miles between Banbury North Junction and Culworth Junction became the heaviest for utilisation of freight in the country for a short section. It was a lone signalman on this section that looked in bewilderment at the rattling of his signal box windows as they vibrated from the air attack on Coventry on November 14, 1940.

What did become essential in World War II, given the unknown extent of air attack and its consequent destruction, was the maximum utilisation of the railways to divert trains, more so than in the first war. The raids in that war of Gotha bombers and Zeppelins was but a prelude to the mass air attack promised by the Nazis and expected by the population in the second. In 1940 connections were made at Reading between SR and GWR; at Oxford between GWR and LMS, who had by now to put aside their days of competition at Oxford with a connection realised between the two stations instead of only a short siding. This was a new double track junction installed just north of Rewley Road station.

A connection at Claydon between LMS and LNER, would enable the east-west route to access not only Calvert brickworks but also the essential Ministry of Food depot established at Quainton Road station, which was supplied by rail. The connection of the former Great Central Railway to the Oxford line at Claydon remains in use to this day by the Landfill trains.

The connection at Bletchley was between the LMS Oxford line and the LMS main line, repeating a former connection of the 1850s when such a curve was intended for use of Worcester trains to access Euston rather than Paddington. It was later removed but was now replaced to allow trains north and south cross-country access.

At Sandy a new connecting line was built between LMS and LNER and put in north of the Oxford - Cambridge line to connect with the former GNR main line, thus giving that line access to the cross-country route.

At Bowes Park between LNER and LNER; at Gospel Oak between LMS and LMS; at Romford between LMS and LNER and at Staines between GWR and SR. Thus were the railways given the option of avoiding the capital and inner precincts of the extended bombing range to reach the southern ports. All things considered, it took some nerve for the crews of trains that had no choice but to go into London and to do so whilst an air raid was in progress. The Luftwaffe always considered trains as prime targets.

A victory in 1945 was a massive relief to the nation and once the jubilant celebrations had died down it was realised that Britain had gained very little from the war besides its salvation.

The railways had worked themselves into the ground. Their thanks was to be described 'as a poor bag off assets' by the Chancellor of the Exchequer Dr Hugh Dalton, MP when nationalised in 1948. How like a serpents tooth was that ingratitude! In some ways what was worse was that wartime astringencies of travelling on the trains by the public either as military personnel or as civilians inflicted a totally unjust publicity damage. People flocked to the new road motor coach companies that advertised cheaper rates and new vehicles.

In 1955 the railway union Associated Society of Locomotive Engineers and Footplate men (ASLEF) with fair justification sought to improve standards for their members that resulted in the conflict of a railway strike, which lasted from May 28 until June 14. It must be said that apart from war it could not have been a more disastrous time to the public. The newly formed British Railways had issued their blue print for the future of the nation's railways on December 1, 1954. This had resulted in a Modernisation Plan in 1955 which included the replacing of steam power with diesel and electric traction. It was intended to spend £1,240 million on the replacement of steam traction with that of electric and diesel. To have continuous braking on all goods wagons which would be organized in new modern marshalling yards. To establish a potential of 100mph on main trunk lines which would cost £210 million to be spent on permanent way. Further, new designs and improvements in coaching stock to safely attain such speeds would cost £285 million. Included in the plan also was the entire rebuilding of Banbury station. The subject and effects of both these occurrences would require the scope of a publication in itself. Sufficient to say that the strike resolved the minds of businesses that had been contemplating the utilisation of road transport. And the master plan proved slow to implement, the enormity of its remit proving difficult against the inertia of a long established industry. It was also mis-guided in policy regarding future freight demands, which Dr Richard Beeching would shake to its foundations a few years later. The public and business were encouraged to think roadways when in October 1959 Ernest Marples became Transport Minister and in November in the same year he opened the first major trunk road, Motorway 1.

Thus the 1960s brought in the devastating effect of the railway system by the much vilified said doctor, but some truths did have to be faced. Even the post grouping companies closed anachronistic stations and the freight system was somewhat ramshackle with poor maintenance of private owner wagons. Plus the time consuming practice of re-marshalling train formations. No system can remain unmodified in perpetuity, the forces of change are unremitting.

Sadly, it is only after the turn of the century to the year 2000 that the railway as a method of travel has become preferred so much again, as, at its best, it has much to offer. This is with apologies to those compressed daily commuters that now have to suffer from years of lack of investment by comparison with that expended on the new motorway road system.

We may now dare to hope for a more integrated transport system.

Marylebone station on June 6, 1966 with very different traction. One of the new diesel multiple units and a steam locomotive alongside it. Very different to the rebuilt Marylebone of the present day where space is utilised to the full and no longer freely available for cars to be parked in the platform area.

H C Casserley

Resisting the Tide of Closure

The nationalisation of the railways came with the new Labour government Act of 1947 to become law from the beginning of 1948. This was grandly proclaimed as 'British Railways' to be operated under a Railway Executive, which was itself under the structure of the British Transport Commission. So the former stock holding companies became six railway regions Western Region, London Midland Region, Eastern Region, North Eastern Region, Scottish Region and Southern Region. The North Eastern Region was merged with the Eastern region in 1967.

To assume that the collective ownership of the railways by central government would bring ordered strategic thinking was a simplistic view. It is a challenge to read Michael Bonavia's superb book *Twilight of British Rail?* (1985) and comprehend, without at least some diagrammatic explanation, the many changes of administration and heads of departments, which makes the brain spin! In the same book he points out the steadily increasing weight of axle loads on haulage vehicles pounding our motorways and ratcheting up repair costs for *all* tax payers. That was in 1985, what of now when at least 40 tons hits the surface, often going to places where they should not! This now, presumably, become part of the governments thinking that heavy goods should be going back to rail rather than building more motorways and the immense liabilities that they incur. The even weight displacement along a train formation makes for smoother and faster propulsion. It was true in 1830s that steel wheels on a steel bearing surface presents less resistant friction and it is no less true now.

Having become part of the LNER the former GCR became included in the Eastern Region which confused the lines of the Joint Committee in British Railways, which later came under the London Midland Region, who showed little enthusiasm for the system.

The former GCR line was further reduced from its once proud hopes and aspirations by being downgraded in January 1960. In 1961 the London Midland Region announced revised services on the former GCR line. On March 4, 1963 closure north of Nottingham which meant a reduction of trains with some semi-fast service retained between Nottingham Victoria and Marylebone. There was a loss also of the overnight services between Marylebone and Manchester. The former GCR lines duplicated LMR at major cities.

In September 1958 the proudly named train 'The Master Cutler', Marylebone to Sheffield, a morning train that returned in the evening, was re-routed from Kings Cross. This train had begun under the LNER in 1947. Another re-routed special train service to Bradford from Marylebone was named the 'South Yorkshireman', started by British Railways in 1948. This also returned in the evening and originally ran over former GCR metals.

Marylebone - Manchester expresses were replaced with three semi-fast trains. Local passenger services ceased on March 4, 1963. The few long distance trains at Marylebone had their stock held in a carriage shed close by on the 'up' side and on sidings at Neasden.

In September 1960 the diesel multiple unit trains the 'Birmingham Pullman' arrived in striking blue livery. Eight-car sets were introduced to run between Paddington and Birmingham and Wolverhampton (Low Level). They were built by Metro-Cammell Carriage & Wagon Company. Hurtling by doleful grubby steam locomotives they inspired images of future aspirations that transpired as a hubris. For their performance did not match their appearance and associated 'Pullman' comfort that they promised. They suffered from a condition all to familiar in early days of regular diesel trains, mechanical failures. This was compounded with inappropriate maintenance facilities and shortage of experienced staff.

The first diesel multiple units designed for local trains ran out of Marylebone on January 23, 1961. Their number increased quite briskly on delivery of new units and installation of maintenance facilities. Units were operating on both main routes to High

Calvert Station looking north in the 1990s with grassy platforms. The line was retained as the route to Claydon Junction for the use of Landfill trains.

Bill Simpson

Wycombe and Aylesbury and a diesel depot was put under construction at Marylebone. They were able to have more effect on the services on the Metropolitan route as the Wycombe line had curvature restrictions and line occupation problems from West Ruislip with the main line connection. Although steam operated goods trains still ran with engines from the sheds at Neasden 14D and Aylesbury, although these were shortly to close down.

The last steam hauled local passenger train from Marylebone via the High Wycombe route was the 11.20 am train on Sunday, June 12, 1961 to Woodford Halse.

The thing of major significance to the railways pending the Beeching cull of 1963 was the Transport Act of 1962, which brought about the dissolution of the British Transport Commission, this became operative on September 1, 1962 following through to 1963. In its place five new boards of transport were established, one being the British Railways Board, British Transport Docks Board, British Waterways Board, London Transport Board, Transport Holding Company also a Regional Railways Board. The essential difference brought to the railways was the removal of fixed charges, which allowed the new Board to fix its own, and the removal of obligations as common carrier. In other words the new Board was to be far more commercially focused as a competitive transport system. A debt of £475 million was written off, and for its first five years would have the support of the Chancellor of the Exchequer to limit its losses up to £450 million. The stage was being set for the doctor to apply his medicine!

The Beeching plan for *The Reshaping*

RESISTING THE TIDE OF CLOSURE

of British Railways was published on March 27, 1963. He was appointed executioner setting out to purge the land of heretical branch lines. The real controversial decision was to smite with all his power upon the former Great Central line north of Claydon Junction to Rugby with total closure. As if this upstart intrusion directed by Watkin's ego was overdue for correction.

The Report stated it thus for closure: London Marylebone-Leicester Central-Nottingham Victoria. With attenuated connections to York, Sheffield and Rugby also gone by May 1969. The much used Banbury-Woodford Halse line went in September 1966 as did Calvert to Rugby.

The London Midland and Eastern Regions gave notice that they were to discontinue all passenger services between Sheffield Victoria and Aylesbury Town and between Woodford Halse and Banbury on April 17, 1966. Temporarily they retained some services between Sheffield Victoria and Woodhouse and between Nottingham Arkwright Street and Rugby Central. Freight services were discontinued in June 1965.

It was all closed on September 5, 1966. The track was removed from the point of the junction with the Oxford - Bletchley at Claydon all the way north with the demolition of such prominent stations of Rugby, Leicester and Nottingham. Its removal was carried out with astounding zeal, as if the contagion of its presence needed to be eradicated! Driving north in 1969 provided a dismal view to see the piles of sleepers and rails on black earth from which they had so recently been ripped. The subsequent removal of the large stations and marshalling yards was awesome in its devastating effect. In reverse, no less an impact than it made during its construction.

The 28 acre goods site at Marylebone was put up for sale at £3,500,000 for housing. It was used as a parcel concentration depot up until the end of 1965 when this facility was moved to Euston. The yard that had opened in April 1999 had suffered bomb damage in 1941 when one section was completely destroyed.

The former GWR route lost most of its stopping passenger services and 'slip' coaches in 1968. It then was made single line from Princes Risborough to Aynho on November 4, 1968. A melancholy time with the retraction of railway services as the timetable would now be encumbered with single line restriction. Princes Risborough to Oxford trains were withdrawn altogether, apart from trip workings to the oil depot at Thame, on January 7, 1963.

Closure for Marylebone could not be included at that stage as it was still operating trains to all stations to Banbury and Aylesbury. But the British Railways Board was keen to find alternatives to the station. The proposals then surfaced for the alternative of routing Aylesbury trains to Amersham, and LT for Baker Street. The closure of the Neasden - Northolt section and the routing of the Wycombe trains to Paddington. It was proposed that the site of Marylebone should become a bus terminus! However this first volley against Marylebone was not allowed to go unchallenged as the Transport Users Consultative Committee protested to the transport minster very strongly that it would cause a great deal of hardship. The Department of the Environment who felt that the consequent hardship caused could not be justified with a question mark over the ability of Paddington to absorb the extra traffic successfully which forestalled this. Any gloom was relieved with the station buffet being refurbished, more eloquently named 'The Regency', and the bar 'The Victoria'. It was reopened on December 14, 1971.

In 1972 north of the station, at the site of the goods yard signal box, a raft of steel girders were erected across the tracks preceding the tunnel mouth to build a 350 bedroom luxury hotel.

Through the 1970s and 1980s the ex GWR, and what was left of the former GCR, system was reduced in form and hope. The slow drip process was gradually undermining the prospects for Marylebone. On March 24, 1974 all passenger trains and freight of the area of Marylebone was transferred from the Western Region to the London Midland Region Control.

The challenge came once more in 1984 when a notice was placed on a poster board on Marylebone station. The proposal was for closure of the following:
  London Marylebone
  Wembley Complex
  Sudbury & Harrow Road
  Sudbury Hill, Harrow
  Northolt Park

London Transport would exclusively supply the following:
  Harrow-on-the-Hill
  Moor Park
  Rickmansworth
  Chorley Wood
  Chalfont & Latimer.

The whole of the service between Sudbury and High Wycombe and London Marylebone to be diverted to and from London Paddington.

It seemed unbelievable, that this inoffensive little terminus with it charming porte cochere was under death sentence, certainly as a railway terminus. Aylesbury trains were to have a shuttle service to Amersham where passengers would have to change for trains on LT into Baker Street. A depressing prospect for commuters.

Finally out of this came a rescue by those that would, like the words of Montgomery at El Alamein, at another railway station, 'not another yard'. There were those that were prepared to fight for a line that was not lost in the preambles of a little used country by way, but a system that ran through high demand commuter country. How fortunate that such dedicated reason was able to prevail.

Given the apathy of the 1970s the

British Railways Board were probably startled at the reaction to their proposed reduction of services into Marylebone station. Which in effect was a writing-on-the-wall for the station. The residents of the district itself and the users of those services managed to coalesce into a potent force that was not lightly to be seen off. The alternative proposal, once again, was to utilise the station area as a coach station as an alternative to Victoria Coach Station and demolish the former Great Central Hotel.

British Rail were under a remit from the government to relieve their annual subsidy by selling off property. There is a certain logic in this as the hundreds of huge Goods Sheds that had been so intensively used throughout the nineteenth and early years of the twentieth century saw their usefulness melt away apart from a lingering survival with National Carriers using a fraction of them.

Although they served the same purpose the opposition to closure had slightly skew motives. There were those that needed the line to be retained as a commuter service and others that were strongly resistant to the plan to convert a large area of the district over to convoys of coaches disembarking their passengers in large amorphous groups with all the attendant disruption of fringe activities. The railway system was by far a more orderly method of transporting large numbers.

British Rail had been struggling for twenty years to get planning permission for the goods yard area that was eventually built on.

There is no doubt that the delay in proceedings by these pressure groups in 1984 saved the situation to a point where demand could not be met by Baker Street or Paddington and Marylebone itself was subject to an increase of use which has continued to this day. The population of London was increasing and so was the use of the railway stations, even in their less than satisfactory condition. Possibly the increase of student population that could not afford cars may have influenced this.

Also a serious and costly modification would be the creating of a separate access to the Bakerloo line (Underground) inside the station area.

Had the protest been less committed and rigorous it is a virtual certainty that Marylebone would have closed.

The bus issue was less secure as an alternative as practical and safety considerations were restrictive to this. The conclusion is therefore that it would have been built over. Sir Peter Parker, the Chairman of British Rail 1976-1983 had strong misgivings on the whole idea on converting railway track beds to bus routes. Sir Peter was a tireless champion resisting closures and deleterious contractions of the service.

The newly established Network SouthEast in 1986 had the right man as Managing Director, Chris Green, whom it transpired did not agree with closure of the station. Neither did the

Rail Users Consultative Committee, the National Union of Railwaymen, Harrow Public Transport Users Association, the St Marylebone Society and several MPs of the constituents involved. They formed effective opposition very quickly. It culminated in the most dramatic change of fortune of any major station. From that time the dismal situation was magically put into reverse. Chris Green made his case against the closure of Marylebone and that a rising demand for rail would produce a new railway concept for commuters. The absurdity of motor coaches was pointed out with the risk for vehicles passing at high speed in tunnels only a few inches apart! The alternatives of Baker Street and Paddington could not effectively absorb the new demand; they also were facing increased pressure. Given the present success of these lines this transpires as a remarkable strength of foresight. Fortunately also there was backing from MPs in the affected constituencies and the general public that were vociferously opposed to the closure of the station. Chris Green and his team won the battle but faced a daunting restoration of the service. Its jointed track, old signalling, dilapidated stations being visited by tired looking diesel multiple units was a very low point of operation. The fact that all of this was overcome in such a triumphant way is as remarkable a piece of railway history as we credit to the achievements of our Victorian champions.

As a curtain raiser during the 1980s steam specials hauled by notable locomotives began to take excursions for tourists to Stratford-upon-Avon almost every weekend and sometimes during the week. Steam enthusiasts could hardly believe this dying flourish of what had once been so dearly cherished. Clearly understood by the lovers of ships and locomotives. It was, however, a grand finale for steam in memorium to former days as the commercial development of the station precluded this continuing and the last steam train ran from there in the late 1980s. But as a publicity exercise it did bring attention to this railway system in a unique way.

To make better use of the station area at Marylebone alterations were made reducing the covered area to two train sheds, which took place in 1991. The Chiltern lines had to be brought up to Network SouthEast standards, which meant investment in virtually every area, so great was its need.

The new network turbos were delivered in 1991, specifically designed for this system of lines.

Chris Green described the diesel depot at Marylebone before modernisation as 'medieval'. It was sold for housing. New line speeds of 75mph instead of 60mph were introduced as new modern track was installed instead of bullhead rail.

All signalling to operate from Marylebone with Automatic Train Protection.

Chris Green went on to be manager of another successful railway brand – InterCity.

On May 30 1952 an experimental three-car ACV railcar set leaves Marylebone as the 13.20 to Princes Risborough. The vehicle underwent trials between Marylebone and Princes Risborough during off peak hours. It had a seating capacity of 129 with 32 seats in the motor car with luggage compartment and Guard. The opposite end car had 45 seats, the middle trailer car had 52 seats. All the vehicles were 40ft in length with an unladen weight of 39 tons 14 cwts. The power unit was an AEC six-cylinder diesel, the same as LT Greenline buses. It had 125 bh with rpm of 1,800 and a top speed of 45 mph. Railway folklore is redolent with graphically applied nicknames and this vehicle became unflatteringly called the 'Flying Brick'.

Neil Sprinks

Stations Along the Line

MARYLEBONE

Having abated the cricket establishment the site for the new terminus station was cleared which involved the displacement of 25,000 of the inconsequential poor. Given the mauling that these settlements had suffered when the Midland Railway came to town with their terminus at St Pancras in 1868 it must have seemed that they were being continually compressed into fewer available hovels. In the fine tuning of historical irony it was the gradual emancipation of this class that would be able to buy cheap workmen's tickets to travel by train and eventually expand into the nascent sprawling suburbs that brought greater patronage of railway services. To what extent the

THE CHILTERN LINE

A GCR train passing West Hampstead in 1901 hauled by a Pollitt GCR 4-2-2 locomotive no 967. This class moved to the Cheshire Lines after 1904.

L&GRP

railway followed its obligation of legislation in 1885 to re-house people seems unclear. Quite possibly only on the occasion where any kind of enforcement could be applied.

However the district was regarded as one of the worst in terms of lawlessness. One Richard Watson the Tollman on the Marylebone toll gate was brutally murdered in his toll house which led to Tollmen being armed.

First passenger trains ran into London on March 15, 1899, the goods traffic on April 11, 1899 and coal traffic began July 25, 1898.

The opening was usual grand affair, the by now cash strapped Great Central Railway probably needed to boost matters as much as possible to know it was open for business. They ran their own omnibus service from Marylebone to Charing Cross and Victoria for continental passengers. The same bus served Waterloo and Paddington.

However, the station never seemed to rise to the prominence of other famous London termini. Possibly an enticement to film producers as several films made use of the station, notably The Beatles in *A Hard Days Night*. And some frustratingly short scenes at the beginning of the film *The Ipcress File*.

The GCR built a huge goods depot adjoining their terminus. They also re-established the old Portman Market

STATIONS ALONG THE LINE

The view looking to the station from the Rossmore Road bridge in 1984 the year of proposed closures.

Bill Simpson

In the late 1980s a train of Mark 1 coaches on the 7.42 am ex-Banbury often hauled by 47s but in this case by a class 50 diesel locomotive at Marylebone.

Bill Simpson

close by the station and built a branch to it in 1901.

The splendid edifice of the Great Central Hotel which remains as Landmark Hotel to this day in front of the station was in fact built by Maples Furnishing Company employing their own architect R W Edis. It had a bicycle track on the roof. The site having been sold to them by the GCR when it was way over extended in its finances on building the London Extension.

During World War I, in November 1916 it became a convalescent home for wounded officers. It became famously known as the headquarters of the British Railway Board until the 1980s.

The station did gain the reputation of being the quietest of the London termini and with its elegant porte cochere it seemed like a station in spa town which gave it a pleasing urbane impression. No less impressive where the trains of GCR with their dining cars and handsome GCR locomotives steaming impatiently at the front.

It was an image that was transferred to the LNER at the grouping when their locomotives also would make an appearance. As explained previously the fate of the station hung in the balance during the doleful 1980s.

Alterations to the station reducing it to two train sheds took place in 1991. But what followed was a greater utilization of space to suit the organization of trains in the twenty-first century.

With the introduction of diesel multiple units and the nadir of steam the London Midland Region, motive power facilities were rationalised and Marylebone MPD became 14D as a sub shed to Neasden which phased out steam with the exception of Engineering Department locomotives.

Further the 28 acre goods yard at Marylebone was advertised for sale in 1962 by British Railways for 3.5 million which included the coal yard which closed at the end of 1965, and other railway properties. The goods depot had suffered heavy damage in World War 2 when one section was completely destroyed. It was proposed that it should be used for housing development.

With the renewed vigour that came with Chiltern Railways franchise the utilisation of space became better organised after much of the site had been sold off. If, as seems to be a certain prospect, the station will be hosting trains from Oxford it would suggest that the terminus will be not such a quiet terminus after all!

Under London Midland Region administration in 1963 Marylebone steam shed was re-coded 1D and (14F).

In 1992 signalling for the entire route was controlled from the Marylebone Signalling Centre with automatic train protection costing 12 million pounds.

STATIONS ALONG THE LINE

What changes! The long view of the station approaches in 1984 with the huge diesel depot, carriage shed and water tower extant also the platform driveway to the bridge on the right. All of which have now been removed, including the signal box.

Bill Simpson

For many years, until the rebuilding of the entire station area in the late 1990s, the GCR turntable survived, probably as it concerned no one rather than for any special consideration. Its hectic days of rotating had long ago ceased by the time this picture was taken.

Bill Simpson

THE CHILTERN LINE

A train from Marylebone to Ruislip Gardens at Neasden hauled by L1 no 9806 in the LNER days of August 14, 1947.

H C Casserley

NEASDEN

The area of Neasden is largely associated with the Metropolitan Railway and London Transport as the former expanded from the city opening its steam shed and coach vehicle sheds on open land, which was how the area was in the later years of the 19-century. With electrification of the Underground the enormous power station was built and opened in 1904 which stayed in use operating on the national grid until 1968. The Neasden shed of the GCR held the steam allocation for Marylebone, which opened in 1899.

With the differences between the Metropolitan and GCR a new connection was made to the GWR at Northolt and opened from Neasden for goods on November 20, 1905, on April 2, 1906 for passenger trains. This gave access to High Wycombe, Princes Risborough, Bicester and Banbury. A signal box situated at Neasden South Junction was opened in the early 1900s and believed closed in 1989. After nationalisation Neasden shed code of the Eastern Region 34E was applied but when it was transferred to the Midland Region for its last four years it became 14D with sub sheds of Aylesbury, Chesham, Marylebone, Rickmansworth. It finally closed in 1962.

Ex GCR D11 Director class 4-4-0 62666 *Zeebrugge* at Neasden shed on Monday evening June 8, 1953 after working two days previously Alan Pegler's *Northern Rubber Special* from Retford to Windsor & Eton; and from Windsor station to Cannonbury (en route to Kings Cross). Until the late 1940s D11s had been daily visitors to Neasden shed. Alongside this is a Neasden based B1 4-6-0 no 61206. The author recalls a visit to Trafford Park shed, Manchester in 1953 and seeing the final days of D10 and D11 'Directors' as they worked out of Manchester Central. Those seen were rather splendidly polished in their lined black, which seemed a fitting memorium to those that carried the names of First World War battlefields.

Neil Sprinks

An N2 0-6-2T on Marylebone - Wembley Stadium special train approaching Neasden South Junction in mid-1950s. The train will continue round the stadium loop and return to Marylebone without reversing. A down Metropolitan electric train T stock Watford line is alongside passing Neasden LT station.

Neil Sprinks

THE CHILTERN LINE

On June 19, 1954 a Southern Railway built H15 4-6-0 30523 approaches Neasden South Junction with a Feltham Yard - Neasden Yard transfer freight train. The train is on the spur from Neasden Junction on the Acton Wells - Dudding Hill - Cricklewood freight line. The tracks on the right lead to Neasden (exGCR) loco depot. On the left are the ex-GCR tracks from Marylebone, and beyond them is the Neasden LT ex Met Rly four track station.

Neil Sprinks

Neasden South Junction signalbox (GCR) on October 11, 1980.

Bill Simpson

Wembley Hill May 13, 1953 showing the northbound *The Master Cutler* being hauled by A3 4-6-2 60108 *Gay Crusader*.

Neil Sprinks

WEMBLEY HILL

Wembley Hill (GCR) station opened on March 1, 1906. Wembley in the mid 19 century was amongst the pleasanter reaches of north London where one could take the air after alighting from the station opened in Pinner Lane in 1842 by the London & Birmingham Railway. From this came the building and expansion of residential properties with a station in May 1844 that was called Sudbury, this later became Wembley Central for Sudbury.

The Metropolitan Railway opened a station in what had eventually become a more populous suburb on October 14, 1893. This came to be known as Wembley Park.

To provide Londoners with a focus to their out of town perambulations construction began of Watkin's tower in 1894 which managed to reach 155 ft to the first platform before it was abandoned, it had been planned to go 1,150 feet. Commercially Londoners did not seem to appreciate the lofty aspirations that were to the gallic taste and it was dismantled in 1907.

The site did of course succeed far more as an exhibition centre with the Great Exhibition of Empire and Industry that opened in April 1924 and continued until October 1925 with a winter break. The stadium built for this became a pantheon of sporting legends as the name 'Wembley' entered English usage as an eponymous accolade of sporting triumph.

The first Football Association Cup Final was played there on April 28, 1923 when the LNER used the loop line for the first time. The final tie of the annual knockout competition was also accorded royal recognition by the Cup being presented by the sovereign. This occasion has now receded into the fabric of the international football calendar. But in the railway period of steam power football was still very much the working mans' weekly respite from the work routine and each May came the pinnacle of its fulfillment, or shattering disappointment, after long anticipation. The teams in the final tie carried immense civic pride as each player was introduced to the monarch. The city or town streets of the competing teams were strangely deserted in the early television age. Vicariously the rest of the nation could participate in this clash of champions after the long struggle through the privations of winter matches. Often the May weather was fine as the hair tingling chorus of 100,000 voices rose and swelled through the mighty stadium before the kick-off. It was an experience, even those not so concerned about football did find very moving.

However, as all things must, the 'modern' styling of its domed twin towers were demolished in 2003. The dust of their collapse must have released faint tremors of so many years of cheering and song as the many sporting legends had been created there. Its replacement reflects the style of its time with an incandescent flourish of hopes and anticipations.

The station situated on the Neasden - Northolt link was originally opened by the GCR and utilised its potential in a very unique way by building an enormous return loop on the site of the Exhibition with its own station for visitors at a half way point, approximately one mile long. This allowed the crowds to arrive and depart within the area of the Exhibition. It came to be known as Wembley Stadium station after the Exhibition closed. This was still in use in the 1960s but was severed to a long siding used only by diesel multiple units before it was finally used in May 18, 1969. It then closed on September 1, track being lifted in 1971. The last major sporting event of its use was the Rugby League Cup Final in May 1968. An interesting use of it in the 1960s was that when the turntable at Marylebone was either occupied or out of use engines would come from the station and use the loop to turn around and go back to pick up their train. Entire trains were also turned on the loop.

The former GCR station was closed on March 28, 1953, this is now replaced with the present station renamed Wembley Complex on May 9, 1978.

Also close by is the considerable complex of Wembley Carriage Depot.

STATIONS ALONG THE LINE

The manifest ambition of Sir Edward Watkin with his tower that reached no further than 155 feet, seen here in 1900. Given that it had been planned to exceed the Eiffel tower it must be regarded as a considerable failure. One to be marginalised in the illustrious career of Sir Benjamin Baker whose Forth Railway Bridge became recognised globally as an engineering triumph.

H M S Lascelles

The 18.34 Marylebone - West Ruislip train calls at Wembley Hill May 13 1953 formed of L1 2-6-4T 67776 (B/F) and two corridor coaches.

Neil Sprinks

THE CHILTERN LINE

An approach to the exotic, there could have been few occasions when LNER 997 N7 tank would arrive at such a setting. The grandeur of asian magnificence that brought to the citizens of the nation a view of an Empire of which they could seldom have personally experienced. Note the condensing pipes on the engine for working on the underground, probably to Moorgate over Widened Lines.

H C Casserley

A photograph of the loop station taken during the Exhibition period on July 4, 1925. Coaches for the 'Never-Stop-Railway' can be seen on the other side of the advertising hordings.

H C Casserley

STATIONS ALONG THE LINE

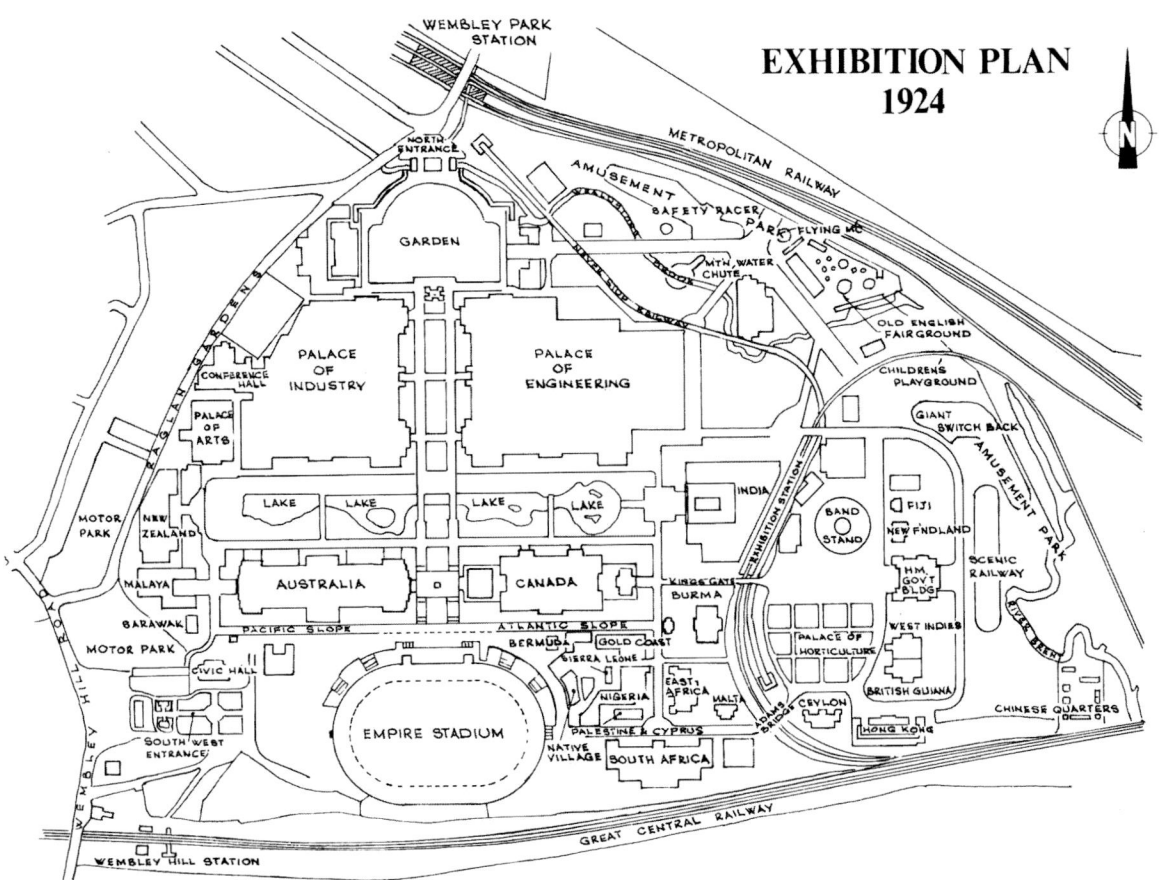

Plan of the British Empire Exhibition 1924.

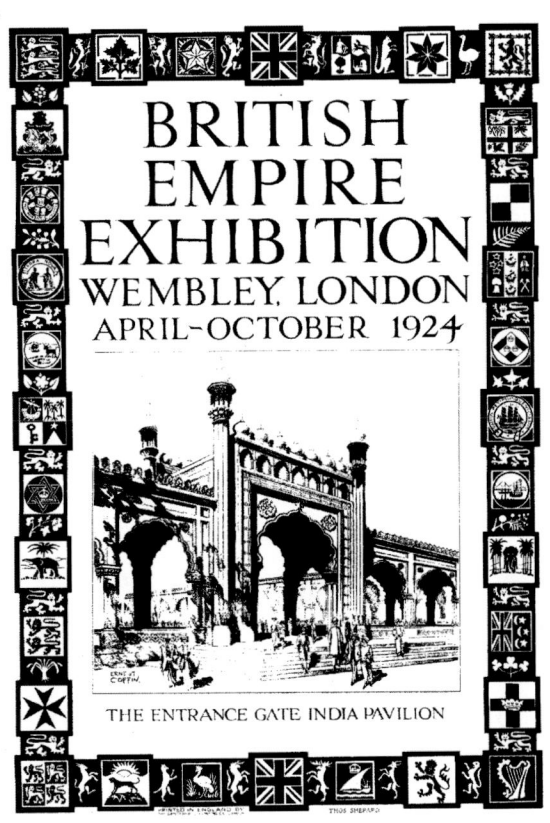

One of the internationally recognised twin towers of Wembley Stadium.

Bill Simpson

Living in the present age when so much is available for the public to be entertained by it is difficult to imagine the value of visiting a fairground. People that never travelled in a car or flew in a plane could enjoy the thrill of accelerated movement for a few minutes.

H C Casserley

The Never-Stop-Railway

Dealing with the flow of large numbers of people in a novel way is often feature of major events. A very interesting feature of the British Empire Exhibition was the Never-Stop-Railway. It was the invention of one Mr W Yorath Lewis, like the present Docklands Railway it was minimally staffed with no driver or conducter, and ran at variable speeds up to a maximum of 24 mph. It was driven electrically by a spiral between the rails which contacted a roller arm underneath each car. Ingeniously at the stations it was closely wound which would of course reduce the speed, between stations it was more widely spaced on the spiral. This form of control obviates the use of brakes.

Each car was 20ft long with seating for 24 passengers and standing for 12.

The railway started at Wembley Park (Metropolitan & LNER Joint) station thence onto an elevated road after passing many exhibits it reached a turning point near the stadium close by the railway station from Wembley Hill. An entire trip would last 10 minutes.

For the Wembley Hill Station entrance, assuming that the passengers were not arriving at the loop station by train, by car for instance, there was a road-rail system with wheel ways of concrete and vehicles hauled by a tractor with rubber tyred wheels.

STATIONS ALONG THE LINE

Turning point for the coaches on the 'Never-Stop-Railway'.

H C Casserley

Conspicuous gradients on the 'Never-Stop-Railway'!

H C Casserley

The 'Never-Stop-Railway at the Exhibition July 4, 1925.

H C Casserley

A faded glory that found no greater future than serving as warehouses and garaging facilities. The Exhibition buildings photographed in 2002.

Bill Simpson

STATIONS ALONG THE LINE

Sudbury Hill (Harrow) June 8 1953 with the northbound *The Master Cutler* in the charge of A3 4-6-2 60051

Neil Sprinks

SUDBURY & HARROW ROAD

Opened in 1906 Four track station with sidings on the 'down' side. Situated on an embankment. Both stations are much reduced from their original structures.

SUDBURY HILL

Originally called South Harrow also four track. Both stations barely a mile apart made distinctive by their locations as Sudbury Hill is in a cutting. Both stations had outstanding of GCR signal boxes

Sudbury Hill looking towards Neasden in the 1960s.

H C Casserley

THE CHILTERN LINE

Sudbury & Harrow Road on July 5, 1960 with a Marylebone - West Ruislip train headed by 42251 Fairburn 2-6-4 tank engine.

H C Casserley

Sudbury Hill, Harrow looking towards High Wycombe on July 5, 1960.

H C Casserley

STATIONS ALONG THE LINE

The 'down' *The Master Cutler* 18.15 from Marylebone to Sheffield (Victoria) joins the GW&GC Joint line at Northolt Junction (South Ruislip station) on July 7, 1954 hauled by B1 4-6-0 61136.
Neil Sprinks

NORTHOLT PARK

Northolt Park opened in 1926 as South Harrow & Roxeth, it changed to its present name in 1929.

At the time of the opening of the British Empire Exhibition (1924) at Wembley colour light signals were installed on the line from Marylebone to Neasden, Northolt and Wembley which permitted passenger trains to follow each other at three minute intervals. This allowed for the closing of Willesden and Canfield Place signal boxes.

SOUTH RUISLIP

South Ruislip originally called Northolt Junction when it opened on May 1, 1908. It Changed to South Ruislip & Northolt Junction on September 12, 1932. It changed to simply South Ruislip on October 6, 1947.

Northolt Park on July 5, 1960.
H C Casserley

THE CHILTERN LINE

West Ruislip on June 14, 1958 as 5012 *Berry Pomeroy Castle* draws in with the 11.30 Oxford to Paddington train. This would have taken the Thame-Princes Risborough route.

H C Casserley

West Ruislip on June 14, 1958 looking north with a train of suburban coaches on the left.

H C Casserley

The Sunday 11.10 Paddington - Birkenhead passing Denham on December 7, 1951 hauled by 4-6-2 Britannia 70017 *Arrow*. The Western Region Britannias later lost the handrails on the smoke deflectors following the Milton accident in November 1955. The last train to Birkenhead train ran in 1967.

Neil Sprinks

DENHAM

Denham is the first station in Buckinghamshire and the name became synonymous with film making with the opening of the studios by Alexander Korda nearby in 1935. From there were created some of the most illustrous British films ever made, *The Stars Look Down, Henry V, In Which We Serve, Brief Encounter, Good Bye Mr Chips,* and many others that had their production based in Denham. It follows that up until the studios made their last film in 1952 that many famous feet must have paced its platforms.

No doubt also Denham Golf Club platform would claim outstanding patronage from its opening on July 22, 1912.

Between Rusilip and Denham is the triangular junction for the Uxbridge High Street branch, which was purely GWR. This opened on May 1, 1907; goods traffic did not begin until May 11, 1914 (see map page 82).

On January 1, 1917 the rail shuttle service between Denham and Uxbridge High Street was withdrawn and replaced with a bus connection.

It re-opened again on May 1, 1919 but closed to passengers on September 25, 1939. It closed to goods in July 1914. Denham goods yard closed on January 6, 1964.

Close by Denham is the Grand Junction Canal.

THE CHILTERN LINE

Denham June 27, 1951 GW& GC Joint 'down' freight ex-WD 2-8-0 90516.

Neil Sprinks

Former GWR 'Prairie' tank 6141 on the 09.45 Good Friday excursion train from High Wycombe to Brighton photographed near Denham Golf Club Halt on the GW&GC Joint line on April 11, 1952. At Kensington Olympia the locomotive handed over the eleven coach train to a Southern Region locomotive.

Neil Sprinks

STATIONS ALONG THE LINE

Denham station April 21, 1963 Looking towards London.
P J Garland Collection

Denham looking north on June 14, 1958. The centre tracks were removed in December 1965.
H C Casserley

Denham photographed from same position in 2014 showing a very different layout of the station. The centre through roads have gone and the 'down' platform face has been reversed. Denham was the one station, apart from Marylebone, on the Chiltern line that was opened as refurbished Network SouthEast station on the same day as the brand was launched at Waterloo.
Bill Simpson

Sunday November 11, 1951 at Denham Golf Club Halt west end. The new 'up' platform is not yet in use.

Neil Sprinks

DENHAM GOLF CLUB

Opened at the behest of the nearby Denham Golf Club in 1912. An attempt to re-name it 'Higher Denham' was thwarted as it defiantly retains it traditional association with the famous Club.

Basic timber platforms, later additionally extended in brick and furnished with little more than the ubiquitous GWR 'pagoda' shelter; which is in itself a triumph of intrinsic charm brought forth from a very basic material.

A comparative view of the halt in 2014 with rebuilt platform surfaces.

Bill Simpson

STATIONS ALONG THE LINE

A Birkenhead - Paddington train thunders through Gerrards Cross with 6014 *King Henry VII* at its head on June, 14, 1958. The ambitions of the Great Western were to introduce such a service and the 'Kings' could be utilised for it, whereas they were restricted from the Oxford route.

H C Casserley

GERRARDS CROSS

To establish the station of Gerrards Cross it required the removal of 1,300,000 tons of spoil in its cutting location. Remarkably the station building was built as a two-storey structure. It became established as the ideal suburban location with good regular rail connection into the capital providing the rarefied contentment of having escaped to the country. This was sampled to the full by the redoubtable General Manager of the Great Central Railway Sir Sam Fay known for his joy of country pursuits. Utilising these rural benefits platform halts were opened by the GWR & GCR Joint Committee. One for Denham Golf Club 1912 that was nearer to London, and one further, at Seer Green opened in 1915. Sir John Betjeman taught at Thorpe House after leaving Oxford.

The station continues in brisk passenger usage to the present day although the goods yard closed on January 6, 1964. This form of traffic had never been the essential purpose of building the line, so the space was utilized for what has become an essential adjunct for passenger traffic – a car park. Further in October 1989 the 'up' line was slewed towards the 'down', the space once used by the through road tracks, allowing the 'up' platform to be widened.

Chiltern Railways traffic intensity was abruptly interrupted in 2005 when a new railway tunnel built to accommodate a new Tesco store collapsed on the line. This interrupted the service from June 30 until August 30.

THE CHILTERN LINE

The station June 14, 1958 looking towards High Wycombe.

H C Casserley

London Midland Region Fowler 2-6-4T 42374 running bunker first leaves Gerrards Cross with the 18.30 ex-Marylebone on June 23, 1954. Obviously considerable use was made of the goods yard at that time.

Neil Sprinks

STATIONS ALONG THE LINE

Gerrards Cross on June 23, 1954 with the 18.15 Marylebone-Sheffield *The Master Cutler* headed by A3 class 60108 *Gay Crusader*.

Neil Sprinks

The tunnel at Gerrards Cross created for the land utilisation of the Tesco supermarket above. The statue of the railway navvy is a fair and overdue recognition of the men that worked hard to build the railways living in hard circumstances, in severe weather conditions and often suffered fatal consequences. Perhaps his iron features formed rueful furrow at the collapse of the new tunnel in June 2005!

THE CHILTERN LINE

Gerrards Cross looking from the 'up' side approach on April 21, 1963,
P J Garland Collection

A steam rail car at Gerrards Cross a very similar example of this type of vehicle now operates at the Didcot Railway Centre. At this time they may have been running a service to Uxbridge.
Real Photographs

STATIONS ALONG THE LINE

Between Gerrards Cross and Seer Green June 7, 1952 the northbound *The Master Cutler* is entrusted to A3 4-6-2 60052 *Prince Palatine*.

Neil Sprinks

SEER GREEN

Seer Green opened April 2, 1906 as a private platform for the Beaconsfield Golf Club. The station opened to public as Beaconsfield Golf Links Halt on January 1, 1915. The name changed again to Seer Green on December 16, 1918; Seer Green & Jordans September 25, 1950; and finally to Seer Green on May 6, 1974.

This continues in a charming nostalgic way to have a GWR 'pagoda' style shelter.

Seer Green station looking in the direction of Marylebone probably in the 1960s.
R M Casserley Collection

THE CHILTERN LINE

Beaconsfield station with a Western diesel approaching with a fitted goods train on April 28, 1964.
R G Nelson Collection

BEACONSFIELD

A station opened on Monday April 2, 1906 along with others at Gerrards Cross, High Wycombe and Princes Risborough. It was recorded with due pomp and ceremony in the columns of the Bucks Free Press.

Surviving GW&GCR notice boards near Seer Green though well weathered, on Friday 20 of July 1951.

Neil Sprinks

It had long passing loops through the platforms and is situated in a cutting. The platforms were extended in 1960. The goods yard closed August 10, 1964.

The through lines that avoided the platforms were removed in December 1973.

The town has a claim to fame in its film studios that produced works by the Crown Film Unit and the GPO Film Unit. From there came the now very famous *Night Mail* a dramatic portrayal of the work of the Travelling Post Office that included the poem by W H Auden and music by Benjamin Britten.

A considerable tiered car park structure has been built in the one time goods yard space.

STATIONS ALONG THE LINE

Beaconsfield looking south with the goods shed extant on the 'up' side on April 28, 1964.
R G Nelson Collection

Beaconsfield station in very different form from its present appearance seen here looking towards London on April 21, 1963.
P J Garland Collection

THE CHILTERN LINE

High Wycombe station in March 1953 the running-in board announces the junction for Marlow and the original branch station of Maidenhead.

Lens of Sutton

HIGH WYCOMBE

The first High Wycombe station of the Wycombe Railway was on a single line with a single platform and an engine turntable on the north side. There were also two lines for a bay on the south side behind the single platform. A goods yard and shed that had its own loop and six sidings.

The new line from Paddington through the Chilterns needed to make some engineering adjustments to some of the route for fast running. North of High Wycombe the route with its steep gradient was re-modelled and excavated anew with a deep cutting through the chalk soil like a wedge in cheese where a second line was built two miles long to ease the gradient. This was part of the High Wycombe to Princes Risborough contract costing £116,797 that was agreed with Mackey & Davis of Cardiff. Work began on this in June 1902.

Appropriate to its name High Wycombe is characteristically a Chiltern town built largely on rising ground in every direction. The early line of the Wycombe Railway circulated the town as if on the rim of an amphitheatre. Across this area an echoing whistle would blast over the town as the steam engine proceeded on its prominent level. This narrow ledge of railway needed to be enlarged with the widening to expand the station and introduce space for quadruple track and sidings facilities in 1906. Cutting further into the hill created a high cur-

STATIONS ALONG THE LINE

High Wycombe station in March 1953 with restrictive sweeping reverse curves.
Lens of Sutton

tain wall on the east side of the station and the platforms were staggered to utilise space further. The curve north of the station forced a restriction of 35 mph.

The prosperity of the town was historically based on furniture construction, which must have been a contributory factor for private railway sidings.

On the north side a timber yard by F Parker and Sons Limited occupied space and a cutting shed. With the yard there was a huge warehouse with rails running alongside.

Also a footpath, footbridge, railway sidings and a stream, another occupier was a William Keen. There were private siding arrangements for Gomme, Broom & Wade Ltd and Wycombe Corporation. Amongst the notables that owned land around the area were the Rothschilds and Disraelis.

A new entrance and circulating area was constructed in 1972 for better access to ticket office windows and the platform with the addition of a Travel Centre for £30.000.

The remarkable feature on visiting the station is to see that the goods shed has survived adorned with an outstanding piece of representative artwork in praise of the ever apotheosized – Brunel.

WEST WYCOMBE

West Wycombe station goods yard was probably very useful until the new yard was built at Bellfield. Given the difficulties of the station at High Wycombe being on a steep hill, which must have restricted horses a great deal, both in hauling goods up and braking on their descent. So it was no great surprise that the GWR&GCR

High Wycombe station on August 14, 1954 with a very grimy 4094 *Dynevor Castle* on a London train.

R K Blencowe

Joint Committee should look to a new yard at Bellfield with six sidings that was very intensely used.

West Wycombe station was listed for closure on November 3, 1958. A strong protest was made to retain the station at West Wycombe and as a result a public enquiry was held by the TUCC at West Wycombe on June 24, 1958. It was claimed by British Transport Commission that the station was making a loss of £2,264 a year. To counter this a West Wycombe station users association was formed to fight the closure, and a petition was signed by 550 users. The crowded buses alternative did not tie in with train times at High Wycombe, which meant that they were not the suggested realistic alternative. Although BTC contested that the buses were not so crowded. They also raised another point in their argument that people could probably drive to Uxbridge and catch the Metropolitan or Piccadily Line trains.

The opposition pointed out that it had always been a popular station for the transport of livestock. This would have had little persuasion as the railway were keen to dispense with this form of conveyance in any case. Historically it would of course have been better for livestock as the access was far easier than the hill position of High Wycombe station.

Nevertheless on November 3, 1958 the station was closed and the area is now a parking space for Heyfordian Coaches. The entrance to the station has been in-filled with new housing. As the area is now even more largely built up it is possible that in the age of Chiltern Line trains it may well have been a facility that could have been well used, had it survived.

STATIONS ALONG THE LINE

The station at West Wycombe, space for double track was never required.
Mike Dewey/Bucks Free Press

The railway on the Saunderton side of the station in the area called Bellfield. The entrance to the extensive goods yard can be seen on the right. In the town below is a factory yard copiously filled with timber.

M Dewey/Bucks Free Press

THE CHILTERN LINE

INDUSTRIES WITH SIDINGS AT HIGH WYCOMBE

Furniture making developed a great deal in the 1840s when people as general consumers began to have some spare money to buy simple furniture. A basic chair called the Windsor Chair was mass produced for this developing market for which other designs followed. The suitability of the terrain around High Wycombe was the extensive beech woods and as the town is situated roughly half way between London and Oxford the carrier wagons could convey the goods in either direction on what would be regarded as a manageable distance for each load.

The 'bodgers' worked in the woods producing spindles and legs that were brought to the manufacturing workshops in the town to be assembled with the seating forms being produced there. The rudimentary methods of the 'bodgers' with hand shaping tools and a lathe operated on a foot peddle with a rotating cord is truly remarkable to see the skilled results from such basic tools.

Therefore the railway was introduced to a an established industry but must have proved a catalyst to its development for at its peak in 1982 High Wycombe had over eighty furniture manufactures operating in the town. The role of the railway tended to be bringing in timber from elsewhere whilst the finished product was handled by road.

An understandable resentment was manifest by the manufacturing company on an occasion when the railway company left new furniture in exposed conditions.

The *Bucks Free Press* of May 4, 1894 reported a dispute between a Mr Edgerley and the GWR over the none release of a cargo of 300 trees due to a payment dispute. The 300 trees were causing traffic disruption around the station. Given the limited space at the original High Wycombe station one can imagine that this was a major problem for all!

E. GOMME & SON

Outstanding amongst the many furniture manufacturing firms was E Gomme who had a siding on the 'down side' beyond the confines of the station near Gordon Road viaduct. This was installed under the provision of a private siding agreement on July 30 1926 between the GWR and the LNER and Ebenezer Gomme, Rupert Gomme and Edwin Gomme of High Wycombe. The siding was linked to the 'down' main line by a trailing connection, the siding points being worked from a two-lever ground frame. The keys to the ground frame were normally kept in the Beaconsfield signal box and when a 'down' goods train called at the siding the guard would collect the keys from the signalman. On arrival the guard would unlock the frame and telephone the signalman at High Wycombe South signal box to say that the train was ready to leave. On arrival the guard would hand the key to the signal man who was responsible in seeing that it was returned to Beaconsfield box by the next available 'up' train. The siding was protected by a gate that was normally kept closed across the line. The siding devided as soon as it was beyond the gate into two parallel spurs built to accommodate eight or nine short wheel base wagons.

Ebenezer Gomme arrived in High Wycombe from Nettlebed, Oxfordshire in the 1880s. He set up a chair workshop beside his house in Totteridge Road. In partnership with Jim Pierce they established Gomme's factory in Leigh Street, High Wycombe in 1909. This factory caught fire in 1922 and was severely damaged. But the partnership was very innovative and they set up another factory in Spring Gardens in 1927 which brought them in direct contact with the railway, thus the private siding in 1926. The company continued to expand and by 1938 they employed 800 people.

Between the wars Gomme's had introduced the concept of a dining room suite that could be expanded as the domestic financial budget would allow. It was an idea that had to be curtailed with the outbreak of the Second World War when Gomme worked on the production of the fuselages for the de Havilland Mosquito aeroplanes.

During World War 2 two designers Barnes and Clinch were appointed to the board by the government to design Utility furniture of dark wood, functional but not given to visual appeal, it was a time of austerity that continued into the 1950s. The modular furniture idea was restored when peace returned and the new post war look was to brighten furnishings with a light wood and sharper colours in upholstery that surpassed the prosaic look of Utility. The designs of 'mix and match' furniture appealed a great deal to customer's whims and budgets. The brand name was G-Plan. The popularity of G-Plan became legendary as the public gave it the generic term 'contemporary'. Gomme opened factories in different parts of the country to meet the high demand.

The company employed over 2000 people and established the patriarchal system of providing accommodation, catering, social and sports facilities that was often structured into large companies.

The chill wind of recession blew into this prosperous enterprise in the early 1980s and the effect was to cause the family owners to sell to a consortium which sold it on to the Hillsdown Group.

The satellite production plants were closed in 1989 and the High Wycombe factory closed in 1992 with the loss of 600 jobs. G Plan continues to be produced by later manufacturers

It is understood that the railway side of things was that raw material was brought in by rail but the finished product went by road. High Wycombe has no rail siding communication at all now.

BROOME & WADE

Broome & Wade became exemplars of the inspired pride and ambition that was evident amongst many individuals in the British nation throughout the nineteenth century. To make and build things carried a high esteem that appeared to become less encouraged in the latter days of the twentieth century. Two apprentice lads with only £5 to their name and a box of tools established a company that would achieve world fame for reliability and quality, even the Germans bought their compressors to build their autobahns because they were so reliable.

Harry Skeet Broome and Jethroe Thomas Wade were apprentices at Paxmans of Colchester but became resteless to take their future in their own hands. The first factory they built was in Lindsey Avenue, High Wycombe. This was 36ft x 16ft and was built by Harry Broome with his own hands in 1898.

They reasoned that the furniture industry at High Wycombe was very labour intensive and would be a good base to introduce their machinery for chair making. In this they were very successful and were able to invent and make machines that got the business thriving and cut costs for the local manufacturers.

When a slump in manufacture did occur they immediately sought to diversify and built motor wagons. But it was the manufacture of compressors from 1910 onwards that really established the company as a household name in the machine tool industry.

They bought a defunct aircraft factory site at Bellfield for £25,000 in 1928 and began to set up for this kind of work. A siding was opened to the site in January 1928 probably in anticipation of machines rolling off the line and to bring in a supply of casting sand, iron and steel. Not only did they build compressors, but they also produced a range of compressor tools for various uses and employed 2000 people in their factory.

In the enlightened understanding that secure contented people make the best workforce they introduced medical and social facilities. They also introduced an annual production bonus.

In 1940 the site needed to be extended by 50% for the production of 'Churchill' tanks and the company began to employ a large number of women.

With the death of Harry Broome in 1958 the company continued but took the form of group status emerging as 'Compair' a new company whereby manufacture was undertaken in a more diversified way and the site at High Wycombe became outmoded for its methods. It was demolished in 1990s.

It is not clear when the siding became redundant but the diesel engine used on it was removed and taken to the Quainton Railway Society site at Quainton in 1978 where it remains.

Saunderton in the early 1960s with a grimy GWR 4-6-0 on a 'down' train.

Andrew Bratton

SAUNDERTON

Saunderton station opened on July 1, 1901 as a single line at first with passing loops. Apparently it was not a success for goods services and these closed on March 1, 1965. It is hoped that passengers were spared the fate of the original station that was destroyed by fire on March 10, 1913 by Suffragettes. The rebuilding with new lines between Saunderton and Princes Risborough probably eased the burden of the locomotives as the gradient was eased from the original of 1 in 88 by the addition of line allowing the 'down' route to be 167, utilising the old 1 in 88 as the 'up' road.

The deep cutting nearby is prone to snow slips, as this is very open country. As such its gentle rolling pastures provide a calming influence of rural peace and seclusion. An enticement to the advertised image of the Chilterns as an ideal destination for walkers.

Modern Saunderton is rather more enclosed but enjoys a regular train service.

Bill Simpson

STATIONS ALONG THE LINE

Saunderton with no 6966 *Witchingham Hall* heading south with a goods train on July 23, 1963.

Andrew Bratton

An 'up' special train headed by no 75075 4MT 4-6-0 BR Standard locomotive. The Southern style head code suggests that it may be bound for somewhere in that region. The date is August 15, 1965, the holiday month!

J F Aylard/Initial Photographics

THE CHILTERN LINE

Class 47 with a well used look hauls a 'down' train through Saunderton in the early sixties.

Prominent along the embankment in this 1955 view of the 16.35 Paddington - Banbury in the approach to Saunderton on the ex-GW & GC Joint being hauled by ex GWR Hall 4-6-0 4977 *Watcombe Hall*.

Neil Sprinks

STATIONS ALONG THE LINE

The unique through train from Oxford to London via Princes Risborough was the 11.25 Oxford - Paddington at Princes Risborough on September 10, 1952 hauled by 'Star' 4-6-0 4053 *Princess Alexandra* with non-corridor coaches.

Neil Sprinks

PRINCES RISBOROUGH

The Princes Risborough - Aylesbury line of the Wycombe Railway extension (Oxford & Aylesbury Act) June 28, 1861 was at first built in the broad gauge when it opened on October 1, 1863.

The Great Western Railway took over the working of the line from February 1, 1867. It was transferred to GWR & GCR Joint Committee from July 1, 1907 Joint Committee track responsibility of 41 miles.

Scott & Middleton did not start work on the line to Aynho until the Joint Committee's line had been fully opened on April 2, 1906. The original single line had restrictive curvature beyond Princes Risborough. The Aynho & Ashendon Junction Railway authorised under GWR

The auto train from Aylesbury approaching Princes Risborough c1930 on this occasion in the charge of one of the GWR 'Metro' tanks.

R S Carpenter

Railways Act of July 11, 1905. This was designed to allow for fast running and laid out by Walter Armstrong, the GWR Works Engineer, who gave it a ruling gradient of 1 in 193 and easing curves to not less than two miles radius.

As described earlier the first Princes Risborough station was on a broad gauge branch of the Wycombe Railway. A modest but sound structure in brick which suggests a certain affluence, for modest country stations where often timber which was used as the cheapest option. The pattern appears to have been the same as the main building at Wheatley. The goods shed was built in timber. By 1870 the line had been converted to standard gauge with branches to Thame, Oxford and Aylesbury.

With the agreements established between the GCR and GWR for Joint undertakings the station needed to be largely rebuilt. This was done from October 22, 1905 and sited 100 yards south of the original site and opened from March 1906.

From that time there were four tracks with 'up' and 'down' in the centre for the fast express trains to pass through, whilst the local and branch trains had their own lines in the platform bays. The improvements also included a pump house with steam pump and a 23,500-gallon water tank. In 1928 electric pumps were installed replacing steam. The original station had to pump water by using a steam locomotive.

Thus it continued through the intensive use of rail travel until closures of the branches, with the exception of the line to Aylesbury. On September 23, 1968 when the 'down' platform was taken out of use

STATIONS ALONG THE LINE

As a result of the LNER assuming responsibility for signalling on the GW&GC Joint line from West Wycombe northwards, GWR signalboxes were to be seen controlling upper-quadrant signals and carrying nameboards on signal box ends. Princes Risborough was a case to point shown here on 14.3.1953 with the 14.40 Oxford-Princes Risborough train alongside headed by 0-4-2T 1442 (painted green and still lettered GWR) with three corridor coaches and a horse box.

Neil Sprinks

altogether. From March 6, 1991 the 'up' non platform track was also removed. The footbridge was removed and the view to rail travellers was to look across at a weedy space with an equally weedy derelict platform on the other side. A prevailing sense of decay.

Thankfully all of that was to change with the new approach in the 1990s and on March 1, 1999 the derelict down platform was opened once again. Rebuilt and restored with glowing new paintwork and a new footbridge for access.

Engine no 6143 approaching Princes Risborough in 1963 with a train of mineral wagons. In December of the same year an engine of this class was unable to restrain the stone train at Bicester and the crew had to jump clear as it toppled over the Launton Road bridge. It was scrapped on site.

J F Aylard/Initial Photographics

The uniform militarism that established the staff structure of early railways is evident in this photograph of GWR staff at Princes Risborough. This is prior to the rebuilding of the station by the GWR&GCR Joint Committee. In the present more relaxed age many members of staff would consider this starched presentation rather excessive for a daily routine! Note the early broad gauge goods shed in the background.

Author's Collection

The 'ploughed field' look at Princes Risborough looking towards Bicester on May 28, 1964. Engine no 6157 has just left the junction onto the Thame branch with an Oxford freight. A caution in bright sunlight as the gentleman crossing will need to take care as the signal close by is 'off' for the 'up' main.

R G Nelson Collection

STATIONS ALONG THE LINE

The age of the Motor Train at Princes Risborough on July 23, 1955 with the 11.36 ex Bicester on the left and 14XX class no 1473 on the 12.05 ex Aylesbury on the right.

H C Casserley.

A class 46 no 46039 arriving at Princes Risborough with the 17.41 ex Paddington, timed to leave Princes Risborough at 18.25 for Birmingham New Street with nine coaches.

G Gamble

Ilmer Halt facing towards Princes Risborough on April 15, 1958.

R M Casserley

ILMER HALT

Whatever service was provided by Ilmer Halt prospective passengers had to choose their trains with some precision as only four 'up' and 'down' trains called in a 24-hour period up until the 1950s when it increased to six each way. The village is at the end of a road of just under a mile from the road between Thame and Princes Risborough and there are only a few dwellings. Nevertheless the GWR apparently believed that a Halt was justified and it was opened April 1, 1929. British Railways had no difficulty in closing it during the Beeching period on January 7, 1963.

The location of Ilmer Halt situated on the minor cul-de-sac road to the village north of Princes Risborough.

Author's Collection

STATIONS ALONG THE LINE

Banbury in the 1980s with A4 class *Sir Nigel Gresley* on *The Shakespeare Limited*, Banbury was a frequent water stop.

A diesel multiple unit in the bay at Oxford in the new Network SouthEast livery.

THE CHILTERN LINE

A pre-1923 map of the railways radiating from north London independently hatched to identify ownership. Note the careful delineation of the section of the GWR&GCR Joint a total of 41 miles.

Author's Collection

STATIONS ALONG THE LINE

Banbury freight yard, or what remained of it in the 1980s. A weedy shadow of its former importance used mainly for storage of faulty or condemned vehicles the decaying remnants of outmoded haulage vehicles. In the 1990s the yard finally was built over with a housing estate.
Bill Simpson

One of the steam specials of the 1980s hauled by the famous *Flying Scotsman* just leaving Princes Risborough.
Bill Simpson

THE CHILTERN LINE

The redoubling of the line between Bicester and Aynho junction in 2002 seen here at a location near Ardley.

Bill Simpson

Railway photographers are a redoubtable breed, hardly likely to be put off by a snowstorm! In this view *Clan Line* is cresting the climb from the junction near the site of Aynho Park Platform. One of them is determined to get the shot, along with the author!

Bill Simpson

STATIONS ALONG THE LINE

Marylebone station in the early 1980s at the time of the publicising of the closure notice. A pall of bleak uncertainty pervades its silent platforms.

Bill Simpson

Drifting exhaust smoke adds some poignancy to the waiting dmu at Marylebone in 1984.

Bill Simpson

THE CHILTERN LINE

Ominous days for Marylebone as diverted services suggest the impending closure of the station. However the red type additional notice pasted on records suspension pending consideration by the London Regional Passengers' Committee. And the extending of the period for lodging objections to October 8, 1984.

Bill Simpson

STATIONS ALONG THE LINE

A new dawn for Chiltern Railways shortly after the re-doubling of the route between Bicester and Aynho Junction.

Bill Simpson

At a slow steady pace for the Western DH *Western Courier* as it rolls over Bicester Town crossing on February 12, 2014 with a special train. It would be the last time that a passenger train would pass over the crossing and through the original station. A week later the line was closed as the crossing was rebuilt for double track and the station was demolished.

Bill Simpson

An illustrated colour guide for the British Empire Exhibition carefully compiled and preserved by Phil Gra...

An outstanding piece of artwork carefully detailed to show railway connections.
Wembley History Society/Brent Archives

THE CHILTERN LINE

The good shed at High Wycombe, a splendid piece of artistry that enlivens an old building in a spectacular way.

Bill Simpson

The Denham Golf Club Halt located in deepest most enclosed Chiltern countryside. It is sometimes a relief to discover bits of the old era in the form of the 'pagoda' shelters.

Bill Simpson

STATIONS ALONG THE LINE

The heritage 'bubble car' in use on the Chinnor & Princes Risborough Railway. The Society can take a great deal of satisfaction, no doubt appreciated by the public, that they not only rescued this line but have successfully recreated the sleepy branch line atmosphere that can now be enjoyed without the cloud of a Beeching contagion!

Bill Simpson

Marylebone in the pre Network SouthEast and Chiltern Railways period, an impression of uncertainty about the future.

Bill Simpson

THE CHILTERN LINE

What looks like a fairly general goods train passes through Ardley station on the 'up' line hauled by 9F no 92245 in October 1959.

Colour-Rail

Tank engine no 6126 departing from Thame station for Oxford on March 23, 1965 with a goods train.

J F Aylard/Initial Photographics

STATIONS ALONG THE LINE

Uniquely welcome, the GWR design pannier tank in British Railway's lined black hauls a special train that has come from Tyseley and is on its way to Princes Risborough and the branch to Chinnor, the location is between Ardley and Bicester in a cutting that is not overburdened with tree cover for once!

Bill Simpson

THE CHILTERN LINE

Although the Watlington branch had few signals it as not prevented the Chinnor and Princes Risborough Railway from restoring an excellent example of the mechanical system signal box. A wonderful attraction to their railway.
Bill Simpson

The GWR style 'pagoda' shelter construction of the ticket office at Denham Golf Club Halt. Which appears now to have been, at least partially, replaced with the machine.
Bill Simpson

STATIONS ALONG THE LINE

The Oxford University Society Railtour, mentioned in the text, calls at Bicester North on Saturday, February 21, 1981.

Bill Simpson

On one of the occasions of the specials it was hauled by V2 2-6-2 *Green Arrow* going south across an area now covered by the M40 motorway south of Banbury.

Bill Simpson

THE CHILTERN LINE

High Wycombe 'up' platform in monsoon style rainfall. A frustration for London bound passengers arriving late for their train is to see it from the 'down' side but have to sprint via the subway to catch it! This platform has now been extended and direct connection will be made with a new footbridge. Probably closing down the un-mourned subway underpass.

Bill Simpson

Princes Risborough station seen from the south. Chilton Railways came into the ownership of DB (Deutsche Bahn) in 2006.

Bill Simpson

STATIONS ALONG THE LINE

Dorton Halt with 7032 *Denbigh Castle* at 16.04 on Saturday July 15, 1961 with a Paddington - Birmingham - Wolverhampton express passing through.

Andrew Bratton

DORTON HALT

Dorton Halt opened on June 21, 1937 between Brill & Ludgershall and Haddenham stations, it cost £374 with its timber shelters. It served a largely agricultural district, Dorton, Wotton, Chilton and Ashendon with a collective population of 650. A novel feature was it being lit with electricity. It closed on January 7, 1963. Rather late in the new auto age to serve nearby Dorton House. The House was a home for the blind during 1939 – 1955 one assumes with many casualties from the recent war. It now serves in the functions business, largely weddings.

A Wolverhampton to Paddington train on July 15, 1961 hauled by 6025 King Henry III emerges from Brill Tunnel Banbury

Andrew Bratton

Haddenham station on April 15, 1956 looking towards Princes Risborough.

R M Casserley

HADDENHAM

Upon Completion of the work by Messrs Nott & Sons Haddenham station was able to open on April 2, 1906. Construction had begun in June 1902, it had cost £170,276 to build this four-track section to Grendon Underwood. Later a private siding was built for a clay works.

The station was unable to resist the burgeoning effect of the auto age of the 1960s and closed to passengers on January 7, 1963. Goods closure had taken place earlier on January 2. The final act of demolition came on April 18, 1966 when both former platform loops were taken out. The whole appearance was diminished still further when the running line was singled in 1968.

However, the needs of the district for rail connection were not lightly to be dismissed and Haddenham & Thame Parkway station opened ¼ mile north of old station site on October 3, 1987 in the new modern style. Thanks to the vigorous promotion of rail travel by Chiltern Railways the need for double track could not be resisted and this was installed once more on July 6, 1998, which required a new 'up' platform to be built with shelters.

New facilities and a ticket office are situated at road level alongside the rail cutting and have extensive car park facilities.

STATIONS ALONG THE LINE

Haddenham station on May 27, 1939 with no 5089 *Westminster Abbey* at the head of a northbound train.

H C Casserley

Crowds assembled at the new Haddenham station to observe what appears to be a goods train about to pass through on the 'up' through line.

Author's Collection

Ashendon Junction train in July 1946 with Castle class no 7007 *Great Western* with a train for Birmingham.

H C Casserley

ASHENDON JUNCTION

The Joint Committee decision to authorise 15 miles of double track line from Princes Risborough to Grendon Underwood was the crucial factor to the GCR. What later transpired as a junction point at Ashendon under the Joint Committee Act of August 1, 1899 gave them their alternative route between Marylebone and the northern cities. The contract was awarded to Messrs. Nutt & Sons.

Before completion the GWR and GCR decided to make the site at Ashendon the limit of the Joint Committee metals and so the 5¾ miles of line to Grendon Underwood became the sole responsibility of the GCR. This was confirmed in the Company's Act of 1907.

It was opened for goods traffic on November 20, 1905 and passenger traffic on April 2, 1906. With the opening of the line to Aynho on July 1, 1910 a signal box called Ashendon North was opened on April 4, 1910 for goods trains, controlling two loop lines with reverse sidings. These loops were removed in 1917, which seems odd as in wartime one would have supposed they would have been needed even more. The signal box closed in 1924.

The connection would have seen an intensity of traffic through most of the twentieth century. More so, when the wartime connection at Claydon was installed. However, with all the changes that came with the 1960s its role was severely downgraded along with the demise of the GCR line that had been its raison d'être.

STATIONS ALONG THE LINE

Ashendon Junction looking north.

H C Casserley

The 'down' line to Grendon Underwood junction was taken out of use on November 28, 1965 following a derailment at Ashendon Junction. What trains services remained used the extant 'up' line until the very last train to run the entire distance, which was on September 4, 1966. Official closure came on July 21, 1967 and the line was severed at the Ashendon end shortly afterwards. Ashendon Junction signal box was taken out of use September 3, 1967. A section of line to Grendon Underwood was retained to serve the private siding of Firman Coates near the site of the old Akeman Street station. These trains continued into the early 1990s.

A view from a train on the 'down' GWR line looking at the former GCR signal box.

H C Casserley

THE CHILTERN LINE

A Great Central Railway warning notice survives at Ashendon Junction on July, 20, 1946.

H C Casserley

A Princes Risborough to Banbury Motor Train passes over the junction hauled by engine no 5407 on July 7, 1946.

H C Casserley

STATIONS ALONG THE LINE

Ashendon Junction signalbox looking north with former GCR line passing beneath the GWR 'up' line on the bridge in the distance on July 20, 1946.

H C Casserley

GRENDON UNDERWOOD

Grendon Underwood Junction, like Culworth Junction, is at the northern end of a valuable connection for the GCR that avoided use of the Metropolitan lines. Locals would need to avail themselves of Calvert station or possibly Brill & Ludgershall if they wished to travel on the railway. The standard pattern GCR signal box was prominently situated in a guarding position of the joining of the lines. Recently the connecting line trackbed has been converted for road usage pending the operation of a new incinerator plant

The new roadway built on the trackbed of the former GCR. Obviously single line working with passing loops!

Bill Simpson

Ex-GWR 5927 *Guild Hall* heads south of Brill & Ludgershall with a London train on June 6, 1964.
Andrew Bratton

BRILL & LUDGERSHALL

The drive of the new railway through Buckinghamshire and Oxfordshire must have made considerable impact accessing village communities that were largely dependent on the very slender road system. This could be particularly difficult in winter. An example of this was the village of Brill south of the new railway. The population made a very strong plea to the Duke of Buckingham to extend his tramway from Wotton to serve the village, albeit along a rickety permanent way. This he did and it was opened there in 1872. Apart from this the village stood in rural isolation on its prominent hill looking across the Vale of Aylesbury.

The village of Ludgershall is closer, north of the line, but smaller than Brill. The station became an unstaffed Halt as early as April 7, 1956. It closed to passengers July 1, 1963 and to goods September 7, 1964. All trace of it as now completely gone.

Close by the line near Brill the Princes Risborough – Aynho line passes beneath the Wotton Tramway (Brill Branch) from Quainton Road to Brill. Here a remote little station of Wood Siding existed.

S W Baker

STATIONS ALONG THE LINE

Brill & Ludgershall on May 31, 1963 with a 'Western' diesel D1007 hauling an express from Paddington to Wolverhampton.

Andrew Bratton

The station Brill & Ludgershall, by appearance not long after completion, looking towards London. A train is about to enter on the platform loop.

Lens of Sutton

Blackthorn is another example of an extensive structure that seems overbuilt for the demands upon its services. It was situated close by the bridge that carried the railway above the (A41) Bicester to Aylesbury road. But it was no great surprise that it should close early on June 8, 1953.

BLACKTHORN

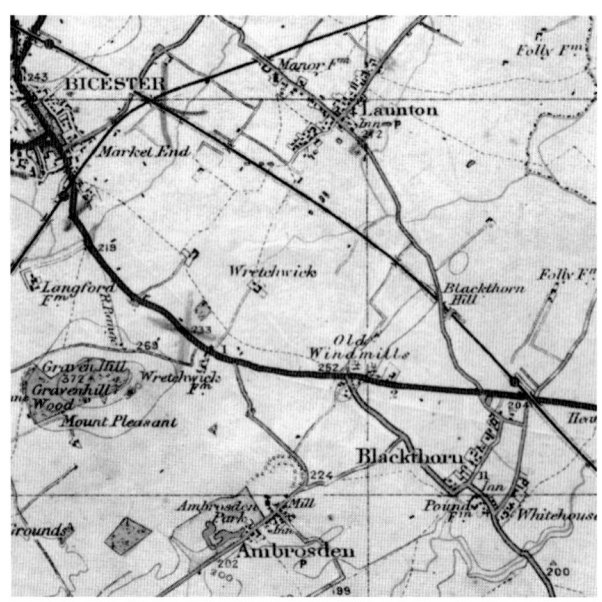

Location of Blackthorn station in relation to Bicester (1914).

Ordnance Survey

With the opening of Blackthorn station it raises in the mind of what expectations the GWR would have for such an impressive station. The village had a modest population of 477 at its peak in 1850 but steadily declined. There were of course all of the farming interests of which a great deal was dairy with milk supply. Of the passenger trains it had at slight variance but not much more than four trains called in each direction per twenty-four hours. The station had two sidings on the 'up' side. It really points up the changing requirements of public service transport before Beeching as an early closure.

STATIONS ALONG THE LINE

Bicester GWR gained from design experience applied to new stations along the line. Dispensing with support obstructions along the platform with the cantilevered roof.

Author's Collection

BICESTER GWR STATION

Since 1850 the town had the railway connection of the Bletchley to Oxford line station (LNWR). In 1862 the line was extended to Cambridge via Bedford which gave good cross-country access for the town. London and the north would require a change at Bletchley.

The building of the new line must have been a striking feature as it was all held on an embankment at Bicester built across all of the roads to the north of the town, it also passed over the LNWR line. The new GWR station was more imposing than the modest limestone building of the LNWR. Four tracks with long platforms and capacious brick built station buildings. It gave direct access to both Birmingham and London.

Continuing north the line climbs to Ardley and crosses the viaducts of Souldern and Aynho until it begins its descent into the valley of the River Cherwell.

The high speed junction connection with the Oxford - Banbury line at Aynho precedes the village of Kings Sutton which had a small but impressive station close beneath the imposing beauty of the tall spire of the village church. Often reflected in the flood plain of the invasive River Cherwell.

The remaining five miles or so to Banbury station lost its rural peace in 1991 when the M40 motorway opened.

THE CHILTERN LINE

A passenger train hauled by a 'Hall' class on June 31, 1964 arriving from the Banbury direction passing on the 'up' through road.

Andrew Bratton

Inspiring images from the famed journeys of L T C Rolt with the gentle purr of his narrow boat *Cressy* meandering through the gathering summer dusk on the Oxford Canal. The passing soft exhaust of a GWR locomotive in glistening green and brass hauling a glowing line of warm lit coaches is a written appreciation of what is lost; as the area is now subjected to the ceaseless roar of modern traffic.

Echoing images from the past a 'Castle' class approaches Ardley with a 'down' special in 2005. With the intensive service of Chiltern Railways on this route such scenes have become comparatively rare in recent years

Bill Simpson

STATIONS ALONG THE LINE

The line between Princes Risborough and Aynho Junction was singled in 1968. With the new franchise and development of the service by Chiltern Railways the route was under pressure for the missing line to be re-instated. This was done in stages, Princes Risborough to Bicester 1998; Bicester to Aynho Junction as seen in the photograph in 2002.

Bill Simpson

One of the special trains that operated over the route in 1992 no 5029 *Nunney Castle* on the re-run of the *Cambrian Coast Express* slows to a halt in Bicester to take water.

Bill Simpson

THE CHILTERN LINE

The point where the Great Western line crosses over the Oxford - Bletchley of the LNWR at Bicester near Tubbs Lane, photographed in 1984. This area is being significantly changed with the building of the new junction link between the two lines as part of Chiltern Railways Evergreen 3 project for the Oxford - Marylebone service.

Bill Simpson

The new embankment begins to grow near Tubbs Lane, Bicester.

Bill Simpson

STATIONS ALONG THE LINE

Ardley station looking south, rather forlorn after closure.
Author's Collection

ARDLEY

Ardley station opened July 1, 1910 close to the road between Oxford and Northampton. A considerable installation in view of the modest sized stations of earlier years. The village of its name was close by and it may well have provided some choice also for the villages of Bucknell and Middleton Stoney.

Significantly a quarry at Ardley had a limestone siding that was supplying stone up until the 1960s. For many years a battered and rust corroded hopper container stood above a similarly rusted siding alongside the line. There were a number of sidings at the station including a loop siding for stone traffic that was quarried close by.

This traffic ceased and the sidings closed some time after the station itself.

It was renamed Ardley Halt on August 1, 1955 which effectively means it became unstaffed. It closed altogether on January 7, 1963.

At the time of writing the rural scale of the location has been subsumed by a structure of immense size and design that looks as if it has landed from an alien world. This is the new incinerator plant on the site of the limestone quarry. Open forums of discussion held for those that sought not to have this monster on their doorsteps were informed of the intensity of 90 ash

Note in this view at Ardley where the steam navvy is working the contractor's railway for taking away the spoil for tipping at another point to form an embankment. This could well have been the space for the station area.

loaded lorries leaving the site each 24 hours. If there is any sincerity in the overtures on needing greener environmental protection, let alone the costs to be inflicted on the road infrastructure, could there not have been a case for covered tracking leading to a re-installation of a siding and moving the stuff away in block trains?

The incinerator company have auctioned the site of the quarry which is now a nature sanctuary.

Close by is the Ardley tunnel of 1144 yards long, this is bored beneath the village of Fritwell that was served with a station on the Oxford-Birmingham line.

One of the Manning Wardle engines used by contractors to build the Great Central Railway and the GWR&GCR Joint line. Robust little saddle tanks that were eventually sold off to small railways all over the country on the completion of the GCR Extension. Three of them were bought by the Oxford & Aylesbury Railway to work on the Brill-Quainton line.

STATIONS ALONG THE LINE

Ardley station under construction in 1907 looking north.
Barry Davis Collection

Ardley station under construction looking south a truly remarkable installation for a village!
Barry Davis Collectionc

THE CHILTERN LINE

The bridge carrying the 'down' line above the Oxford – Banbury- Birmingham line. This was considered for removal when the Chiltern line was singled.

Bill Simpson

One of the 'Shakespeare' specials in the mid-1980s hauled by 4-6-2 locomotive *Clan Line* about to cross the girder bridge over the Oxford – Banbury line seen from the Oxford Canal.

Bill Simpson

Aynho Junction in the 1980s, when the signal box was undergoing repairs. Not many years later it was demolished. The Bicester 'up' and 'down' lines are on each side of the Oxford - Birmingham lines in the centre.

Bill Simpson

AYNHO

The GWR opened Aynho Park Platform on July 1, 1910; it was lightly built on an embankment, with an attractive chalet like appearance. The ideal location of a tree enclosed country station that one likes to think of in the fullness of warm summer sunshine, but judging by the timetable it must have had many rain soaked grey silent Monday afternoons as well when it was ignored by most passing trains; with the exception of three stopping trains each way. The brick built ticket office was situated at the foot of the embankment alongside the Aynho to Deddington Road. A pathway with railings was laid out on both sides of the line.

Presumably responsibility for it would come under the Stationmaster of the station on the Oxford to Banbury line that was close by.

Aynho Park Platform closed with the last train on Saturday, January 5, 1963; the *Banbury Guardian* reported it in the issue of the 10th of that month. The Reporter Douglas Golby duly wrote that Aynho was fortunate in having another station, an alternative not to be appreciated for very long as that also closed on November 11, 1964. He pointed out the familiar death sentence of costing with an annual loss of £7000, which would be relieved by its closure. The last train was a three-coach diesel multiple unit leaving for Princes Risborough, this had an unfamiliar large crowd on the occasion

The 1920s or 1930s, a GWR train is about to cross the Deddington to Aynho village road. On the right is the gated footpath to the 'down' platform. The entrance to the 'up' is on the other side of the embankment alongside the brick built ticket office.
Author's Collection

The last days of semaphore signals at Aynho Junction as a class 50 passes through in 1988.
Bill Simpson

to ride the last train from there. To be fair the station had been little used as it never seemed to exceed its three daily trains in all its lifetime. Which begs the question that fewer available trains means less attraction to regular passengers. Or would more stopping trains encourage greater use? Given the time of the sixties when the great ambition of all was to own one's own transport, probably not. Although it is a conundrum that has been hotly contested for many years subsequently. The station and buildings on the embankment were demolished in 1964, shortly after closure. The brick built ticket office survived in dereliction until quite recently.

STATIONS ALONG THE LINE

The Aynho Park station with single diesel unit no W55002 arriving with the 11.15 Banbury to Princes Risborough service on September 4, 1962.

Andrew Bratton

Aynho Park station on Wednesday, September 5 1962 with no 6005 *King George II* hauling a Birkenhead - Paddington train passing through.

Andrew Bratton

THE CHILTERN LINE

Time to replenish water as *Swansea Castle* no 7008 passes over Aynho water troughs on Monday July 22, 1963 with a Paddington - Banbury stopping train. The junction for the Oxford and Bicester lines is beyond the bridge in the distance.

Andrew Bratton

Two 'Director' class engines *Zeebrugge* and *Somme* on the *Farnborough Flyer* (Leeds-Farnborough) a special train organised by the late Alan Pegler passing near Aynho on Sunday, September 11, 1955. The train was hauled from Leeds to Doncaster by 60133 *Persimmon.* At that point the two 'Directors' took over and continued to Basingstoke where a Southern Region class N15X took the train forward to Farnborough. By all accounts it was an exhilarating day and a triumphant flourish to the final days of these engines.

Peter Waylett

STATIONS ALONG THE LINE

A steam special in the late 1960s prior to singleing hauled by 4-6-0 no 7029 *Clun Castle* passing between two mounds of earth that had until comparitively recently supported the platforms of Aynho Park Platform.

Between Ardley Tunnel and Kings Sutton are two viaducts, one at Souldern, seen here, and another at Aynho.

Bill Simpson

THE CHILTERN LINE

A Castle class 5076 *Gladiator* pauses on a summer day in July 1964 with a stopping train from Paddington via Bicester to Banbury.

Andrew Bratton

KINGS SUTTON

This station remains still as the only intermediate stopping point between Aynho Junction and Banbury. Kings Sutton was opened June 1, 1872. It became an unstaffed Halt in 1951. The footbridge was removed which then left passengers the only option of crossing the tracks on the clearance from a red light to green on the Banbury end of the platforms. This precarious procedure is now gratifyingly restored to safer traditional method of a new footbridge that was installed in the 1990s.

The station buildings, that were modest but impressive in appearance, were demolished soon after 1963 apart from the 'down' side shelter, when it became an unstaffed Halt.

The buildings related in style to the other GWR station on the line from Princes Risborough to Aylesbury at Little Kimble.

As mentioned earlier the station is overlooked by a truly remarkable village church. Its steeple marking its location for many miles around.

Between King Sutton and Banbury was a signal box and sidings both called Astrop.

STATIONS ALONG THE LINE

Kings Sutton station in the early 1960s with a special hauled by a 'Castle' class heading south.
Andrew Bratton

With the distinctive spire of Kings Sutton church in the distance 4959 *Purley Hall* progresses with a mixed train through bright early evening sunlight on Thursday June 30, 1964.
Andrew Bratton

THE CHILTERN LINE

Banbury station on the occasion of the first train from Banbury to Bicester. One of the 'Metro' tanks which is working a Motor Train service which no doubt would call at the newly built Aynho Park Platform. The station had 'Brunel' design all-over roof that was removed in the early 1950s at a time when extensive rebuilding took place that was completed in 1958.

Photo Archive, Oxfordshire County Council

BANBURY GWR STATION

The GWR station at Banbury was opened on September 2 1850, in the broad gauge, it became mixed gauge in 1852. There had been some conflict between the LNWR and the GWR railways continuing beyond Banbury, the latter proving to be successful. The LNWR did arrive a few months earlier on May 1, 1850. Between them was built the local gasworks through which both stations were connected with a gas siding, and an exchange siding.

Powers to build the Woodford - Banbury line were obtained in 1897; it was opened in August 1900. With the building of the new line and the connection to Woodford the goods facilities became greatly expanded with a capacious goods yards at each end and with much larger steam sheds. In the 1930s the yard at Banbury became a 'hump' marshalling yard. Some GCR engines and trains ran through to Banbury and across the North Junction link to reach Culworth Junction and onto the GCR main line. An arrangement conceded to the GCR from the GWR over the latters metals from Ashendon Junction.

Trains that ran from Banbury yard were the fast class C perishable freight trains of the GWR to Acton that usually

The elegant lines of the GWR Castle class survived in exemplary form in preservation with special trains operating from Didcot to Birmingham as in this view in early 1980s of *Drysllwyn Castle (Earl Bathurst)*.

Bill Simpson

travelled late at night. There was also a great deal of stone traffic.

On the passenger side a motor train service was introduced between Banbury, Bicester and Princes Risborough with three stops at Aynho Park Platform.

During the Second World War the lines of the GWR&GCR Joint may well have seen their heaviest traffic ever, with the essential roles contributed by the connections at Ashendon Junction to Grendon Underwood and Banbury to Culworth Junction to Woodford.

Many through trains ran to the north and south coast, an example was the York - Bournemouth that was taken over by a Banbury crew as far as Reading.

By contrast with being such an intensive railway junction the connections at Banbury were subject to the Beeching Report as it closed down the ex-GCR main line and consequently brought to an end a large part of the traffic.

In 1965 eight 'Britannias' were allocated to Banbury steam shed that saw out their last days of the main line operation between Banbury and Marylebone. Their trains often only four coaches long. Probably about all they could manage, as they were allocated to Banbury after the steam sheds closed on the ex-GCR main line. But they were in such bad condition Banbury was happy to get rid of them to Scotland and revert back to their well-favoured Black Five engines. These worked services along with grime saddened 'Halls' until the last days of the steam shed which closed in 1966. The station continued as a diesel depot until 1984.

THE CHILTERN LINE

Banbury GWR steam shed was intensely busy supplying motive power for a busy main line with trains to Birmingham and Wolverhampton, and exchanging of engines on long distance through trains. These included the lines to Woodford, and Bicester. There was also the line to Cheltenham via Chipping Norton line with much ironstone traffic. So Banbury was no sleepy backwater, in this view during the 1960s one of the 'Royal Scot' class engines no 46156 *The South Wales Borderer* is in attendance. The closure of the steam shed in 1966 disintegrated a whole social system of working people.

Andrew Bratton

Banbury Marshalling yard closed down from its role as being on the circuit of the nations marshalling yards on May 4, 1970 leaving a small section of the North End yard still in use. As mentioned, decline had started with the closure of the line to Woodford Halse. Also the yard ceased to be used by the ore trains from the Wroxton Ironstone Company. It continued to be used to store old wagons and the occasional 'cripple' removed from a passing train. The 08 diesel shunter remained to carry out a reduced role until the middle 1980s. At the beginning of 21 century the site was cleared completely and houses were built over it.

Steam locomotives became part of life associations for many people and an absorbing passion for some. They were encouraged by the skill of storytellers *La Bette Humaine* (Emile Zola) *Brief Encounter* (Noel Coward) *Murder on the Orient Express* (Agatha Christie) *Dr Zhivago* (Boris Pasternak); the list goes on and could easily fill a page. Consequently when the inevitable time came they were cast aside, ungratefully; awaiting their fate encrusted in dirt and grime at the end of some remote siding. This was in such a contrast to their high glory days. Thankfully it is part of the British national character not to accept such final ignominy and for a time the route between Marylebone and Stratford-upon-Avon, passing through Banbury, gave witness to this determination as rescued steam locomotives proudly hurled forth in liveried splendour. Their shrill valedictory whistles echoing through the wooded Chilterns and across the Cherwell Valley.

STATIONS ALONG THE LINE

A class 47 waits at the head of a train at Banbury in the 1980s in the period when modern diesels were seen hauling the old 4-wheel goods stock of the steam period.

Bill Simpson

A class 47 heads south from Banbury in 1988. The train is passing over the place where now the M40 motorway crosses the line. The crane in the fields on the right is laying pipes as preparation for the motorway construction to begin.

Bill Simpson

The Wotton GCR signalbox shortly after the opening of the new station.
Alfred Cadle

WOTTON

A Decision was taken to build stations at Wotton and Akeman Street in latter half of 1904. Webster & Cannon built these for £1,514.

The stations on the link line are something of a puzzle in terms of patronage. What could the GCR expect in populous along those long bare timber platforms? A sparse settlement at Wotton Underwood was dominated by the large manorial dwelling of the third Duke of Buckingham, one time chairman of the LNWR. Upon his passing on March 26, 1889 his nephew Earl Temple inherited and ran the estate with its attendant six-mile tramway connection to Quainton Road station and Brill. The GCR had to build a plate girder bridge above this at Wotton. They also built quite fine station buildings in brick at road level, which are now privately occupied. These look across to a group of estate cottages that once housed workers serving the Tramway, all evidence of which has long since ceased to exist apart from the stable building that endures in a rickety sort of way for farm storage.

Wotton House itself appeared also to fall on hard times and was eventually rescued by the late Mrs Brunner and survives in splendid appreciation in its secluded woodland confines, especially the north and south pavilions.

The Wotton station of the GCR did marginally better than its neighbour station at Akeman Street as it closed to both passengers and goods on December 7, 1953.

STATIONS ALONG THE LINE

The bridge over the one time Wotton Tramway photographed in the 1960s.
H C Casserley

A model of Wotton on the Brill Tramway by Mile End Methodist Model Railway Club shows the bridge of the GCR passing over the tramway.
Bill Simpson

THE CHILTERN LINE

Very few photographs exist of the remote station of Akeman Street but this clearly shows much of the station which had quite a short lifespan as a passenger station. The station building has survived as a private house.

Lens of Sutton Collection

AKEMAN STREET

The station at Akeman Street, apart from its grandly appropriated Roman name could have hoped for little in terms of passenger use as the nearest concentration of population was the small village of Westcott to the south and Grendon Underwood and Edgcott north, the latter may have found Marsh Gibbon on the Oxford - Bletchley line a greater advantage.

The station buildings were built at road level and opened on April 2, 1906.

They remain still, situated alongside the Bicester and Aylesbury road (A41), which was crossed by a bridge.

The station was an early casualty in terms of closures that were brought in during the 1930s by the post grouping companies. It closed to passengers on July 7, 1930.

Goods traffic proved a little more durable as it lasted until January 6, 1964, this is with the exception of a private siding for fertiliser trains, which ran on until the early 1990s. The track has now been removed and the surface is in the process of being transformed into a road for the use of lorries to run to the new incinerator plant being built near Grendon Underwood. This has brought about a replacement with a modern structure of the bridge seen at the beginning of the 'Introduction' chapter in this book. This bridge was built by the GCR over a country lane between Quainton and Edgcott. The bridge over the A41 was removed some time after the closure to goods.

STATIONS ALONG THE LINE

The 13.12 'Parliamentary' stopping train from Nottingham to Marylebone leaving Calvert, the last station on the GCR London Extension line, on April 22, 1953 behind A3 4-6-2 60111 *Enterprise*. The train, routed via the Met & GCR Joint line, will stop next at Quianton Road.

Neil Sprinks

CALVERT

Calvert remains as an access point to the Landfill site of the one time brick making plant of the Itter Brick Company that later became part of the London Brick Company. The last brick train from the works was on December 6, 1977. The tall chimneys that had for so long been incongruously conspicuous in this rural location fell into their own brick dust a few years later.

The works opened in 1900 as the works of A W Itter, it was connected with sidings to the GCR and a siding that was almost a branch line to the LNWR Oxford and Bletchley line at Claydon, this was about a mile in length. At the junction there was a signalbox called 'Itters Sidings'. Those with knowledge of this siding remarked that it seemed very poorly laid and wagons tended rise and fall with the ground surface from the ancient 'strip' farming. The works was fortuitously placed for serving two railway outlets but the GCR was the one that dominated with 100 brick wagons per day passing from the works onto their line.

A W Itter sought to expand the manufacture of bricks. He established his first works at Kings Dyke, then sought out land to build another to expand his business further, importantly with good railway access.

He chose Steeple Claydon in Buckinghamshire as a site close to the Oxford to Bletchley line and also where the new Great Central line crossed over. He bought land there from Lincoln College, Oxford and opened the Calvert works in 1900. This enabled him to supply bricks for the extensions to these railways and to London.

The railways were crucial to the growth of the brick making industry that was centred at Peterborough at the eastern end of the long Oxford Clay belt. Originally brickworks developed in a small way to supply local districts owing to cartage difficulties. What changed things significantly was the development of what became known as the 'Fletton Process', a means of mass-producing bricks. This was due to the unique properties of Oxford Clay that could be pressed and fired with a certain degree of self-combustion which aided and cheapened the process of firing them. Cost effectively this had to be done on a large scale with rows of pressing machines, so without the railways this would not have been possible. The firing was carried out using a specially designed kiln called the Hoffman Kiln, this was a large single storey structure with partitioned chambers, these were sealed after stacking. The fire was on a circuit rotating through holes in the walls of each chamber in which the bricks where placed, this was aided with coal slack fed from openings above as it continuously rotated. As the bricks had combustible properties there was a concentration of carbonated residue displaced in the firing which had to be drawn off; thus the high chimneys that were built on the kilns seen at Calvert. But also seen at Newton Longville, Bletchley, Ridgmont, Lidlington, Millbrook, Wotton Pillinge, Kempston Hardwick, in fact near stations all along the Oxford - Bedford route.

There was a demand later for bricks for the building of the extensions to the Morris Motor Car factory at Oxford which was supplied by rail using this link.

There is no doubt that the industry enjoyed a long period of prosperity and high demand continuously seeking labour for the many plants. A superb example of the 'model village' was built at Wotton Pillinge (Stewartby) in the 1930s with all social amenities made available to the workforce in an erudite consideration for their welfare.

Originally there were many individually owned works that used the process but they were all gradually absorbed into the London Brick Company. From that time on the brick production industry had its peaks and troughs until the whole concept of the manufacture became very dated in terms of producing a cleaner environment. Areas near the factories tended to be heavily coated in dust residue and the continuous odour from the many chimneys suggested a pollutant factor.

To continue the process at all would require enormous investment in

STATIONS ALONG THE LINE

Permanent way men pause for the photograph at the Calvert in the Great Central Railway days.
Author's Collection

alternative processes which was not considered viable. All of the works gradually closed down from the 1970s onwards to 1994.

Calvert station closed to passengers March 4, 1963, the last passenger train calling there on September 5, 1966. A shrinkage of railway services as a precursor of eventual closure came with the introduction of the bus service from Steeple Claydon and Aylesbury calling at Calvert to replace local train services in 1963. Further in the same year trains from the north to Marylebone ran from Bletchley to Claydon Junction where they connected with the ex-GCR main line and went south to Marylebone over the wartime connection.

However the angular shape of the container lifting derrick that now dominates the view was introduced with Landfill contract of 1980 to bring London domestic rubbish to be dumped into the deep pits that had yielded millions of bricks for so many years. Close by the grassy platform of the station seems reminiscent of an ancient monument in its crumbling form rather then its abandonment as recently as 1966.

Undoubtedly it was the securing of the Landfill contract with British Rail to run their rubbish trains to the new siding that saved the line north of Aylesbury from complete closure.

THE CHILTERN LINE

The railway siding entrance to the works used to connect with the Great Central Railway. Note the menial shelter allocated for pointsman for the lever operation nearby.

Bill Simpson

The Calvert brickworks locos: L/15 0-4-0DM Fowler 22895/1940 and 4-wheel DM Motor Rail (Simplex) 9922/1959. Photographed in 1978 close to one of the Hoffman system kilns

Bill Simpson

STATIONS ALONG THE LINE

A railway on the top of one of the kilns that carried the fine coal fuel that was placed in heaps near to the lids that are lifted to feed the coal into the fire chamber below.

Bill Simpson

Steam locomotive used at Calvert up until the introduction of diesel traction. An Aveling & Porter Well Tank that was nicknamed 'The Pig'. A locomotive of this type is preserved at the Buckinghamshire Railway Centre at Quainton.

R M Casserley

Rather basic but well used Monks Risborough & Whiteleaf Halt on June 6, 1960.
H C Casserley

MONKS RISBOROUGH

Monks Risborough and Whiteleaf Halt opened November 11, 1929. It was renamed Monks Risborough on May 6, 1974. It seemed a little awkward perched in its position close to the bridge where the road to Chinnor passed under the line. This precariousness was proved in 1985 when it collapsed. However the passenger use must have been sufficient for it to be replaced on a less elevated site 132 yards to the north. This opened on January 13, 1986. The line has always been quite intensively used by schoolchildren.

The 18.50 to Aylesbury leaves Princes Risborough on May 6, 1953, the auto coach being hauled by ex-GWR 0-6-0PT 3694 running bunker first. An up main line train is in the adjacent platform on the right.
Neil Sprinks

STATIONS ALONG THE LINE

Pannier tank no 6403 heading for Princes Risborough with the 13.25 ex Aylesbury train on a sunny June 4, in 1960.

H C Casserley

The Halt in the summer of 1987. This was the structure that eventually collapsed, the shelter would only keep out *some* rain!

Bill Simpson

Little Kimble in winter, February 21, 1964 looking towards Princes Risborough.

Peter E Baughan

LITTLE KIMBLE

Although it never had any goods sidings or other railway facilities Little Kimble was given a very presentable station building when it opened on June 1, 1872. The simple dimensions of the building were set off with some distinctive ornamentation by the original chimneys.

As a station it ceased to provide staff facilities during the 1960s, and is now a simple Halt platform for the commuter service. The station building is now a private house. For those that wish to know such things the GWR running-in sign is now in the Museum at the Buckinghamshire Railway Centre.

Little Kimble, sleepily burdened with a hot day in August 1985.

Bill Simpson

STATIONS ALONG THE LINE

A building similar to that of Kings Sutton, Little Kimble station, according to the holiday posters in 1938. This view looking towards Aylesbury.

Author's Collection

Little Kimble, the typical country station, though only as a modest Halt, on September 13, 1958.

R M Casserley

South Aylesbury Halt in the 1930s.

Author's Collection

SOUTH AYLESBURY HALT

South Aylesbury Halt opened February 13, 1933 to serve nearby factories and Southcourt housing estate. It closed on June 5, 1967. It tended to be used for visitors to Stoke Mandeville hospital.

In view of the recent infill of new housing it may now be feasible to install a stopping place near this point.

South Aylesbury Halt looking towards Aylesbury on September 28, 1963.

Peter E Baughan

STATIONS ALONG THE LINE

The 12.40 Princes Risborough - Aylesbury train approaches Aylesbury off the GWR & GCR branch on November 2, 1953 formed of one ex-GWR Auto coaches propelled by 0-4-2T 1411 running bunker first.

Neil Sprinks

AYLESBURY

What began as a minor broad gauge branch line terminus of the GWR in 1863 did develop into a situation where all railways in north Bucks lead to the town. The first railway had arrived as a branch from the London & Birmingham main line in 1839 (see *The Aylesbury Railway* OPC 1989). The promotion of a railway from the town to join with the Oxford – Bletchley line was promoted in 1863 by the Aylesbury & Buckingham Railway but struggled to find financial support.

It did manage somewhat tenuously to gain enough to open the line on September 23, 1868. Rather compliantly, as it transpired, the GWR converted their line from Princes Risborough to standard gauge. This meant that the A&B could compound an agreement with the GWR to run their line also. They could not afford engines and rolling stock themselves. With only three trains daily they were unlikely to gain much revenue from the line and it is at the behest of the

THE CHILTERN LINE

A Freight train from Princes Risborough arrives at Aylesbury on the afternoon of May 6, 1953 hauled by ex-GCR 'N5' 0-6-2T 69369. To the left of the GCR Aylesbury South signal box is the Met & GCR Joint line from Baker Street, Marylebone and Harrow-on-the-Hill. Aylesbury North Signal box of similar design was on the north side of the Met & GC Joint line as it continued beyond Aylesbury Station towards Quainton Road (and the north of England over the GCR London Extension line).

Neil Sprinks

GWR that they managed to survive long enough to find salvation in the ambitions of the Metropolitan Railway that bought the line in 1891. The Aylesbury station was rebuilt on the arrival of the Metropolitan in 1886.

The climax of all this advancement in the town's railway expansion came with the opening of the Great Central Railway's extension south in 1899.

Civic development made Aylesbury the county town in 1740 and canal and railway communications greatly supported this as it expanded into surrounding countryside. Although lines north have withered away to freight only, Chiltern Railways have greatly developed the lines south to London both on the one time Met&GCR lines and the original branch to Princes Risborough. If the East – West Railway proposal to connect once more to the Oxford – Bletchley line north is realized Aylesbury's significance will again be established in railway communications. As a branch of this is to be developed from Claydon Junction.

STATIONS ALONG THE LINE

A view of the west side of Aylesbury station in the early Summer of 1949 shows a Western Region train probably bound for Paddington, awaiting to depart from the platform usually used by Princes Risborough line trains. In the shed yard are two ex-GCR tank locomotives L3 2-6-4T E9053 left and N5 0-6-2T E9300.

Neil Sprinks

On April 22, 1953 the 1.00 pm Western Region train from Paddington arrives at its destination, Aylesbury behind locomotive 2-6-2T 6160. This Saturday train left the Western main line at Maidenhead and was routed via Bourne End joining the GW&GC line at High Wycombe to continue via Princes Risborough.

Neil Sprinks

Chinnor station, the building that was demolished but rebuilt by Chinnor and Princes Risborough Railway.

THE WATLINGTON BRANCH

Chinnor was the first station along the branch to Watlington and thanks to volunteers one to survive. The cement works close by ensured the branch survival beyond the closure in 1957. This began with lime production in the latter part of the nineteenth century and moved on to cement production in 1928. A sidings was added and coal and gypsum were brought in from the east midlands. Every month, 400 wagons of coal and 1,300 tons of gypsum, the kind of bulk haulage done so well by the railways. After the First World War much of the produce from the factory went by rail. Lime production ceased in 1974.

This was a line that sadly pre-empted the work of the 'Doctor' as its last passenger train ran on Saturday, June 29, 1957. Such a line would always be vulnerable to road competition and the freight service followed, beyond Chinnor, on January 2, 1961.

But for the Chinnor & Princes Risborough Railway preservation group all would have faded completely after the closure of the cement works in 2000. Quite the reverse is the case, the Society now operates a regular service of trains along 3.5 miles of railway and with admirable dedication have completely rebuilt the architectural gem of a station with its chapel like gables and now run their own services. They have had number of occasions to celebrate like in 2010 when, with no little organisational skill, they were able to bring an 0-6-0 Pannier Tank from Tyseley, no 9600 came back onto the branch on a fine sunny July day. This was to haul the 'Centenary Express' which was diesel hauled between Tyseley and Banbury, then steam to Princes Risborough and Chinnor. On return a class 47 'Royal Train' style ran ahead of the triumphant little black pannier back to Banbury.

STATIONS ALONG THE LINE

The 15.05 Watlington - Princes Risborough approaching its destination station on March 14, 1953 with ex-GWR 0-6-0PT 4691 bunker first hauling an auto coach. A GWR signal is off for this train whereas behind it can be discerned the LNER upper quadrant for the adjacent track, the GWR Wycombe Railway line from Oxford via Thame. This as a result of the LNER having responsibility for signalling on the GW&GC Joint line through Prince Risborough.

Neil Sprinks

Contrast in fixed distant signals on approach to Princes Risborough as a result of the LNER take over of GWR&GCR Joint line signalling for High Wycombe northwards i.e. including Princes Risborough north box to whose signals these distance relate: LNER style upper quad on the single track ex-GWR line from Oxford and Thame. With GWR style lower quad on the ex-GWR Watlington branch. Far distant in the Chiltern Hills is Whiteleaf Cross. This photograph taken on March 14, 1953.
Neil Sprinks

THE CHILTERN LINE

A class 47 no 47099 leaves Chinnor for Princes Risborough with empties from the cement works. At this time the station buildings had been demolished, they stood immediately to the right of the loco. This view on April 8, 1982.

G Gamble

A North British type 2 loco no D6358 shunts a train of coal and gypsum wagons into the Chinnor cement works sidings.

G Gamble

STATIONS ALONG THE LINE

The rebuilt station at Chinnor by the Chinnor & Princes Risborough Railway. A remarkable achievement superbly completed.

Bill Simpson

Aston Rowant looking towards Princes Risborough on October 14, 1957. A repeat of the very picturesque style of station buildings characteristic of this line.

R M Casserley

THE CHILTERN LINE

An extra coach is included in this view of pannier tank no 4650 at Chinnor.

Peter Waylett

WATLINGTON

The station for Watlington opened on August 15, 1872 and was some distance from the small market town that no doubt provided good business for carrier carts. Its compact assembly of a country branch line terminus has always proved an ideal subject for model railway enthusiasts.

The station is of the same attractive pattern as the others on the branch with a goods shed, originally a locomotive shed with essential coal and water facilities. It also had a carriage shed.

The branch was operated on the one-engine-steam system with few signals on its length, apart from those at Princes Risborough. At Kingston Crossing there was a fixed distant and at Shireburn for Watlington station. There was also a signal box at Watlington with a 'home' signal for facing points at the goods yard, and an 'up' starter. Sidings were released by the train crew using the electric train staff.

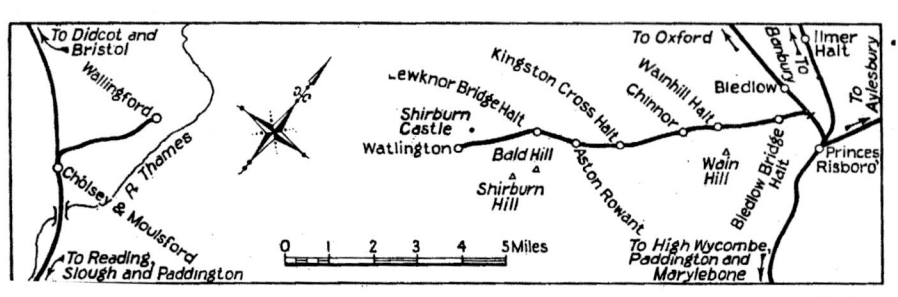

The branch line of 8 miles 66 chains that was cut back to Chinnor in January 1961.

Railway Magazine.

STATIONS ALONG THE LINE

The daily train on the Watlington branch with pannier tank and auto coach in the early 1960s.
Peter Waylett

Train at Watlington in the early 1960s.
Peter Waylett

Watlington the complete branch line terminus; station buildings, goods shed, cattle facilities, coaling platform and shelter on the right for the branch train.

Bledlow station on the branch to Thame, the corrugated building on the right is now used as the TPO store at the Buckinghamshire Railway Centre.

STATIONS ALONG THE LINE

Thame, like Banbury, retained its 'Brunel' design all over station roof well into the twentieth century. A welcome advantage for passengers sheltering from the vagaries of English weather.
R M Casserley

THAME

Opened originally as a terminus of the Wycombe Railway on August 1, 1862 with single track in the broad gauge, this was later converted to standard in 1870. It became a through station to Kennington Junction and Oxford in October 24, 1864.

Thame became well known as a cattle market town that developed further with the opening of the railway. Extra cattle pens were built in 1931. Surprisingly although it provided an alternative pathway for Oxford trains from those via Reading and Didcot it was only occasionally used as such.

Extra traffic for this branch came from the opening of the car works at Cowley in 1912, regular daily trains of new cars passed down the line into Oxford. This remains in use and could serve as new urban rail connection. There was new traffic in 1958 when the oil terminal opened at Thame.

The passenger services on the line were withdrawn in 1963. Freight continued until 1967. The exception being 5¾ miles of track from Princes Risborough that continued with oil terminal trains until 1991.

As a public amenity the route has now been re-opened as a footpath, cycle path and bridle way named 'The Phoenix Trail'.

THE CHILTERN LINE

The 10.00 am Oxford to Princes Risborough one mile north of Thame on April 24, 1953. This ex-GWR 2-6-2 tank no 6111 61XX was the locomotive that conveyed the last passenger train on the branch in January 1963.

Peter Waylett

Former GWR 'Prairie' 6126 arrives at Thame on March 23, 1965 from Princes Risborough. The inclusion of the signal box forms a good photographic composition.

J F Aylard/Initial Photographics

STATIONS ALONG THE LINE

Chalcombe Road platform opened April 11, 1911. About four miles from Banbury it served the village of the same name until its closure on February 6, 1956.

CHALCOMBE ROAD

The final days of the former GCR route with the York – Bournemouth south of Woodford hauled by a class 37. The train used the link to Banbury and on to Oxford.

Allan Baker

Eydon Road the 12.30 Woodford Halse -Banbury stopping trian at Eydon Road Halt on May 6, 1953. The three-car corridor train being hauled by ex-GCR 0-6-0 64369 tender first (J11 Class). The gentleman seated on the left appears to be enjoying a sunlit break in his labours.

Neil Sprinks

EYDON HALT

Eydon Road platform opened on October 1, 1913 about eight miles out from Banbury on the important link between Banbury and Culworth Junction which was 8¼ miles long. Goods and minerals began running on the link on June 1, 1900. This meant that the GCR could now cease to run freight trains to the GWR via Quainton Road and Aylesbury. Passenger services began on August 13, 1900 with trains between Oxford and Leicester.

The Halt would probably prove useful to the local village of its name close by and for farm produce. With its attendant signalman it lived out is rote of seasons until British Railways decided in the pre-Beeching era that it was no longer needed and it closed on April 2, 1956.

The new Marylebone, fresh bright colours, electronic train indicators and a wholly dynamic presentation of an efficient railway terminus. With the arrival of Oxford trains it will achieve something close to the fulfillment that was hoped for one hundred and sixteen years ago.
Bill Simpson

Beyond the New Horizon

There are many phrases that one might borrow to describe the extreme turning point of a critical situation, commonly understood. Most of them could therefore be applied to the situation of Marylebone station and the Chiltern Line from 1984 onwards with notice of closure of stations and diversion of services until 1986 when the first glimmer of hope came to the embattled and redoubtable defenders.

Increasing population, many being students that could not afford cars, began to use the railways more and the arrival of a totally reorganised system made using them much easier.

The situation in the 1970s and early 1980s was of a railway system heavily subsidised by the government with a focus almost entirely on how this could be reduced. Post Beeching railways might have survived but it was a lingering endurance. The Serpell Report was published in 1983 which seemed to be a form of euthanasia for most of the system. Fortunately this rang alarms in the right quarters. As far as the Chiltern services were concerned it may not have been realised but a turning point had been reached.

As early as 1972 the prospect of buses replacing trains at Marylebone

THE CHILTERN LINE

was seriously projected. This was against a railway system that was very much on the defensive, Beeching had been only ten years previous and the effect on investment and morale continued to decline. However opposition was marshalled against the suggestion and it is beyond the scope of this book to cover this as it is an extended and highly detailed story.

But in terms of the Chiltern line's story the leadership of Chris Green, the new energetic manager of BR who had revitalised Scottish railways with a new brand called 'ScotRail' was asked by the Chairman of The Railways Board, Bob Reid, to come and do a ScotRail in the South East as his work had been so successful in Scotland. It can easily be imagined by anyone that knew the railway system in that region at that time of what an immense challenge this was. The story of how this was achieved and its development that lead to the reversal of a decline in railway investment and patronage is told in great detail with enlightening text and illustrations in *The Network SouthEast Story 1982-2014* by Chris Green & Mike Vincent, Oxford Publishing Co (2014). In this book the dire truth is revealed when the advertising agency for Network SouthEast, J Walter-Thomson, refused at first to take on the railway in its existing form as it had such a run down appearance. However the book clearly provides the narrative of how this was overcome and Network SouthEast was indeed launched on June 10, 1986.

Chris Green made the highly evocative statement that ' a railway does not have to be drab' which was saying a great deal where the Chiltern lines were concerned. The visual transformation was selected with studious care and produced an impression of bright optimism that matched the aspirations of the future.

The region of 'Network SouthEast' was divided into six sub-sections.

South East
South Central
South Western
West
East
North

The Chiltern line was included in the North sector.

What is clear is that the new railway that became NSE established all the new thinking that prevails still in the franchise undertaking of the present day in what is now Chiltern Railways. The optimism of new trains on the drawing board arriving at rebuilt and redecorated stations with everything painted in bright new colours that stimulated public appeal. The slam-door DMUs had to be retained until replacement trains came off the production line but even they emerged with this new look and were cleaned on a regular basis. Digital clocks appeared on platforms on overhanging posts that were very legible and easily seen from a considerable distance.

Also, and of essential importance, the staff of the entire system were infused with the confidence that if they played their part in maintaining the new standards they would have a secure job with competitive pay.

The result was that by 1992 when privatisation was announced the system was handed over to privatisation franchises with zero subsidy. What had been achieved by the time that NSE closed 1993/94 from 1982 was miraculous and provided the new franchise companies with a positive and lucrative base on which to build the future. The baton has clearly been taken up on the Chiltern Line where new trains and extensive station facilities, car parks and regular services have proved very successful.

Fortunately driven by a man of Chris Greens ability, Adrian Shooter, managing director of Chiltern Railways.

The Chiltern line was initially included in the north sector of NSE but later won its freedom as a new Thames & Chiltern Sub Sector from 1989.

The essential message to keep the newly refurbished stations clean and tidy also was established by NSE. In terms of teamwork, application and passenger appeal the period from 1986 to 1989 can be regarded as a golden age of railway transformation when the government subsidy for a system with perceived lack of demand was completely reversed leading to the expansion that has not lessened to the present day.

The introduction of one day Capital Cards and Network Cards that later amalgamated with London Transport as Travelcard to make a bus and tube available on one fare spectacularly freed up the off peak utilisation of train stock and generated a new income source which targeted families and groups. This was creating the right message about rail travel as being an 'in' thing to do and passenger numbers started to rise.

The commuter patronage grew in an alpine rise on the graph analysis between 1983 and 1990. Chris Green pointed out to the government 'that if all London commuters came by car the queue would stretch 800 miles to the Orkneys!'

On successful conclusion of the negotiated franchise for the system the new Chiltern Railways (M40 Trains) became effective from July 21, 1996, continuing the progress that NSE had started. This was manifest in projects named; Pre-Evergreen, Evergreen 1, Evergreen 2 and Evergreen 3. The first brought about the re-doubling of track between Princes Risborough and Bicester in 1998 with higher speeds, also extra platforms at Princes Risborough and Haddenham & Thame Parkway. Evergreen 1 in 2001 brought a doubling of track between Bicester and Aynho Junction, in effect re-installing double track on the entire route. Evergreen 2 facilitated all of this route capacity increase with a new stock depot built at Wembley in 2002 and extra platforms at Marylebone with improved signalling. Evergreen 3 has proved already to bring a dramatic

THE CHILTERN LINE

The new double track crossing of the Oxford - Bletchley line at Bicester in June 2014.
Bill Simpson

enhancement with 100 mph line speeds and the remodelling of the junctions at Neasden (70mph) and Aynho (85mph) and is continuing at the time of writing with the new Oxford service under construction.

Essential for the commuter increase large expansive car parking facilities have been constructed at all of the stations. An important point being that there is always likely to be space available, no matter how late one arrives, in the peaks of a working week.

At the time of writing the bus terminus spectre has been raised once more which is a challenging prospect to imagine. The station appears most of the time to be heavily used with trains shuttling back and forth over both Chiltern lines and with the Oxford service in prospect being added to with a connection to Milton Keynes.

One assumes this will bring a high demand for platform space. In September 2015 the new Oxford Parkway – Marylebone service is to be opened.

A published booklet by East West Rail, which is committed to open the Oxford to Cambridge railway once more, also advertises a new semi-fast service from Milton Keynes to Aylesbury Parkway and Aylesbury duplicating other services from Princes Risborough to Marylebone. On the evidence of rail usage at present and particularly the pressures on the Oxford district one can easily conclude that both these new services will draw on a considerable catchment area. It follows therefore that the facility of Marylebone in development of track usage will be considerable, prohibiting any alternative transport structure, ie buses.

BEYOND THE NEW HORIZON

On February 9, 2014 a special train hauled by *Western Courier* hauled a very interesting railtour that ran over former GWR&GCR lines to Marylebone. The route took it through both stations at Bicester. In so doing it was the last passenger train to pass over the road crossing at Bicester (LNWR). It is seen in the photograph having just emerged from Ardley tunnel going south.

Bill Simpson

An effective view of the new briskness of the Chiltern Railways service. Since the re-doubling of the track the timetable has increased the number of train journeys with an intensity probably greater than the days of the GWR!

Bill Simpson

FURTHER READING

A History of the Great Central, George Dow Vol 1 (1959); Vol 2 1962; Vol 3 1965. Locomotive Publishing
The Great Western & Great Central Joint Railway, Stanley C Jenkins (2006) Oakwood Press
A History of the Metropolitan Railway Volumes 2 & 3, Bill Simpson (2004) Lamplight Publications
Quainon Road Station and Other Stations in the Vale of Aylesbury, Bill Simpson, Lamplight Publications
The Network SouthEast Story 1982-2014, Chris Green and Mike Vincent, (2014) Oxford Publishing Company
The Wycombe Railway (Part 1), C L Mowat, The Railway Magazine, September 1933
The Wycombe Railway (Part 2), C L Mowat, The Railway Magazine, November 1933
Great Central Railway's London Extension, Robert Rothbotham (1999) Ian Allan Publishing
Paddington to Princes Risborough, Vic Mitchell and Keith Smith (2002) Middleton Press
Princes Risborough to Banbury, Vic Mitchell and Keith Smith (2002) Middleton Press

INDEX

Acton 122
Acton & Wycombe Railway 17
Acton Wells 42
A Hard Days Night 36
Akeman Street 92, 101, 126, 127
Amersham 31, 32
American 17
Annesley 10
Ardley 92-3, 107-8, 111-3, 119, 157
Ardley Halt 111
Armstrong, Walter 19, 76
Ashendon 13, 16, 19, 97
Ashendon Junction 100-3, 123
Associated Society of Locomotive Engineers & Footplate Men (ASLEF) 26
Aston Rowant 145
Astrop 120
Auden, W H 24, 64
Aylesbury 6, 16-7, 29, 30-2, 40, 75-6, 92, 104, 106, 120, 128, 131, 134-5, 137-41, 156
Aylesbury & Buckingham Railway 18, 139
Aylesbury Parkway 156
Aynho 6, 16, 31, 100, 104, 155
Aynho & Ashendon Junction Railway 19
Aynho Park Platform 84, 115, 117, 119, 122-3
Baker, Sir Benjamin 45
Baker Street 9-10, 31-4, 140
Banbury 23, 25, 27, 31, 40, 74, 81, 83, 95, 102, 107-8, 114-5, 117-8, 120, 122, 123-4, 125, 142, 149, 151-2
Banbury Guardian 115
Banbury North 14, 25
Barnes 70
Basingstoke 118
Beaconsfield 64-5, 70
Beaconsfield Golf Club 63
Bedford 107, 130
Beeching, Dr Richard 27, 30, 80, 91, 106, 123, 152-3, 154
Bellfield 67, 68, 69, 71
Berne Conference Gauge 11, 15
Betjeman, Sir John 59
Bicester 11, 40, 78-9, 84, 87, 92-3, 95, 106-7, 109-10, 118, 120, 122-4, 128, 155, 157
Birkenhead 16, 17, 55, 59, 117
Birmingham 6, 17, 29, 97, 100, 112, 114-5, 123-4
Birmingham (New Street) 79
'Birmingham Pullman' 29
Blackthorn 106
Bledlow 148

Bletchley 26, 31, 107, 110, 128-9, 130-1, 139-40, 156
Bonavia, Michael 28
Bourne End 141
Bournemouth 151
Bowes Park 26
Boyes, Graham 10
Bradshaws 14
Bradford 14, 29
Brief Encounter 124
Brill 13, 97, 103-4
Brill & Ludgershall 104-5
Brill Tramway 127
Britain 26
Bristol 14
British Empire Exhibition 43, 47-8, 53, 88
British Rail 33, 131
British Railways 26, 28-9, 38, 80, 93, 152
British Railways Board 30-2, 38
British Railways Modernisation Plan 25
British Transport Commission 28, 30, 68
British Transport Docks Board 30
Britten, Benjamin 64
Broom, Harry Skeet 71
Broom & Wade 67, 71
'Brunel' 122, 149
Brunner, Mrs 126
Buckinghamshire 5, 10-11, 55, 104, 130
Buckingham, Duke of 104, 126
Buckinghamshire Railway 8
Buckinghamshire Railway Centre 133, 136, 148
Bucknell 111
Calvert 26, 30, 103, 129-32, 133
Cambrian Coast Express 109
Cambridge 6, 26, 107
Canfield Place 10, 53
Cannonbury 41
Capital Cards 155
Cardiff 19, 66
Catesby 13
'Centenary Express' 142
Chalcombe Road 151
Channel Tunnel 10, 11
Charing Cross 36
Cheddington 16
Cheltenham 124
Cherwell, River 107, 124
Cherwell Valley 124
Chesham 40
Chiltern Hills 6, 9, 15, 34, 66, 72, 124-3, 153

Chiltern Railways 6, 38, 59, 87, 91, 98, 108-10, 140, 154-5, 157
Chilton 97
Chinnor 17, 93, 134, 142, 144-6
Chinnor & Princes Risborough Railway 91, 94, 142, 145
Chipping Norton 124
Chorley Wood 32
'Churchill' Tank 71
Circle Line 9
Claydon 26, 30-1, 100, 129
Claydon Junction 131
Clinch 70
Colchester 71
Compair 71
Consett 14
Coventry 25
Cowley 149
Cressy 108
Crown Film Unit 64
Cricklewood 42
Culworth Junction 14, 25, 103, 122-3, 152
Dalton, MP, Sir Hugh 26
Deddington 115, 116
de Havilland 70
Denham 55-7
Denham Golf Club 56, 58-9, 90, 94
Derbyshire 14
Didcot 17, 123, 149
Didcot Railway Centre 62
Disraeli 67
Docklands Railway 48
Doncaster 118
Dorton Halt 97
Dorton House 97
Dr Zhivago 124
Dudding Hill 42
Eastern Region 28-9, 31, 40
Edgcott 5, 128
Edgerley, Mr 70
East –West Rail 6, 140, 156
Edis, R W 38
Eiffel Tower 45
El Alamein 32
England 8
Eton 41
Eydon Halt 152
Euston 16, 26
Evergreen, Pre- 155
Evergreen 1 155
Evergreen 2 155

158

INDEX

Evergreen 3 6, 110
Farnborough 118
Farnborough Flyer 118
Fay, Sir Sam 17, 23, 59
Firman Coates 101
'Fletton Process' 130
Football Association 44
General Post Office 64
Gerrards Cross 59, 60-4
Germans 71
Gomme & Son, E 67, 70, 71
Gomme, Rupert 70
Gomme, Edwin 70
Goodbye Mr Chips 55
Gordon Road 70
Golby, Douglas 115
Gospel Oak 26
Gotha Bombers 25
Grand Junction Canal 55
Grant, Phil, 88
G-Plan 71
Great Central Hotel 33, 38
Great Central Railway 6, 10-1, 14, 16, 19, 20-6, 29, 31-2, 36, 38-41, 44, 59, 76, 100-3, 122-3, 126-32
Great Eastern Railway 24
Great Exhibition of Empire and Industry 43
Great Northern Railway 8-10, 14, 24, 26
Great Western Railway 6, 8, 16-7, 19, 20-1, 24-5, 31-2, 58-9, 63, 70, 75-8, 80, 93-4, 100, 106-8, 110, 115-6, 120, 122-4, 134, 136, 139-40, 143, 150, 157
Great Western & Great Central Joint Committee 5, 6, 16, 19, 21, 23-4, 29, 53, 56, 59, 63, 67, 75, 77, 78, 81, 100, 123, 141, 143, 157
Green, Chris 33-4, 154-5
Greenline Buses 35
Grendon Underwood 5, 17, 19, 98, 100-3, 123, 128
Grimsby 8, 14
Haddenham 19, 97-9
Haddenham & Thame Parkway 98, 155
Harrow-on-the-Hill 32, 140
Harrow Public Transport Users Association 33
Helmdon 20
Henry V 55
Hertfordshire 11
Heyfordian Coaches 68
High Wycombe 16, 19, 29-2, 40, 52, 56, 60, 64, 66-8, 70, 71, 90, 96, 143
Hilsdown group 71
Hoffman Kiln 130, 132
High Speed Line 2
Hull 14
Ilmer Halt 80
Immingham 23
Inter-City 34
In Which We Serve 55
Itter, A W 129
Itter Brick Co 129
Itter's Sidings 129
Journal of the Railway & Canal Historical Society 10
Keen, William 67
Kempston Hardwick 130
Kennington Junction 17
Kensington Olympia 56
Kings Sutton 107, 120-1, 137
Kitchener, Lord (Kitchener's Army) 24
Kings Cross 9, 24, 29, 41
Kings Dyke 129
Kingswood 13

Korda, Alexander 55
La Bette Humaine 124
Labour Party 28
Landfill 26, 30, 129, 131
Landmark Hotel 38
Leeds 118
Leicestershire 11
Leigh Street 70
Lewis, Mr W Yorath 48
Lidlington 130
Lincolnshire 8
Lincoln College 130
Lindsey Avenue 71
Little Kimble 120, 136-7

Locomotives:
ACV Railcar 35

0-4-0
Aveling Porter WT 133

0-4-2T
Metro Tank 76; 14XX (1442) 77; (1473) 79; 'Metro'122; (1411)139

4-4-0 'Directors' 6; 23; (62666) *Zeebrugge* 41; (62667) *Somme/Zeebrugge* 118

4-4-2
Pollitt 'Single' 36

4-4-2 Robinson 'Atlantics' 6, 23

0-6-0 Pannier Tank 9600, 79; 93; (5407) 102; (3694) 134; (6403) 135; (9600) 142; (4691) 143; (4650) 146; 147

0-6-0ST MW 13; *Cyprus* 112

0-6-0
J11 (64369) 152

0-6-2T
N2 41; N7 (997) 46; N5 (69369) 140; N5 (E9300) 141

2-6-2
V2 (60800) *Green Arrow* 95

2-6-2T Prairie 61XX
(6141) 56; (6160) 141; (6111) 150

2-6-4T
Fairburn (42251) 52; L3 (E9053) 141;Fowler (42374) 60

4-6-0:
Black Five, (44920) 4;
King Class, 6; (6014) *King Henry VII* 59; (6005) *King George II* 117; (6025) 97
Castle Class, 16; (5012) *Berry Pomeroy Castle* 54; (4094) *Dynevor Castle* 68; (5029) *Nunney Castle* 109; (7032) *Denbigh Castle* 97; (5089) *Westminster Abbey* 99; (7007) *Great Western* 100; (7008) *Swansea Castle* 118; (7029) *Clun Castle* 119; (5076) *Gladiator* 120:121; (5051) *Drysllwyn Castle/Earl Bathurst* 123
Robinson, 25
B1 (61136) 53
Hall, 72; (6966) *Witchingham Hall* 73; (4977) *Watcombe Hall* 74; (5927) *Guild Hall* 104; (4959) *Purley Hall* 121
Star, (4053) *Princes Risborough* 75
N15X 118

'Royal Scot' (46156) *The South Wales Borderer* 124

4-6-2
A3, (60108) *Gay Crusader* 43; (60051) *Blink Bonny* 51; (60108) *Gay Crusader* 61; (60052) *Prince Palatine* 63; (60103) *Flying Scotsman* 83; (60111) *Enterprise* 129
A4 (4498) *Sir Nigel Gresley* 81
Merchant Navy *Clan Line* 84, 114
Britannia *Arrow* 55; 123

2-8-0
WD Austerity (90516) 56

2-10-0 (92245) 92
(Steam Railcar) 62

Diesels:
Class 50 37; 116
'Western' DH 64; (D1062) 87; (D1007) *Western Talisman* 105; *Western Courier* 157
Class 46 DE (46039) 79
NB Type 2 (D6358) 144
Class 47 125; (47099) 144
Class 37 151
0-4-0 Fowler DM 132
4-wheel Simplex 132
DMU: 81; 85; 91; 117

EMU:
T stock 41

Loans & Guarantees Act 1929 25
London 6, 8-10, 15-6, 23, 33, 36, 38, 59, 70, 75, 105 107, 130, 131
London & Birmingham Railway 6, 8, 43, 139
London Brick Company 129, 130
London Extension 8, 10, 140
London Midland & Scottish Railway 24-6
London Midland Region 28-9, 31-2, 38, 40
London & North Eastern Railway 24-6, 29, 38, 44-5, 70, 77, 143
London & North Western Railway 11, 17, 24, 107, 110, 122, 124, 126, 129, 157
London Regional Passengers' Committee 86
London Transport 31-2, 40, 42, 155
Ludgershall 97, 103-4
Luftwaffe 26
Lutterworth 9, 10
Mackey & Davies 19
Mackillop, G H 19
Maidenhead 16, 66, 141
Manchester 14, 19, 29, 41
Manchester, Sheffield & Lincolnshire Railway 6, 8-11, 23
Mansfield 23
Maples Furnishing Company 38
Marlow 66
Marples, Ernest, MP 27
Marsh Gibbon 128
Making of a Railway 13
Marylebone 4-8, 10-11, 14, 19, 24, 28-36, 38, 40-2, 44-5, 52-3, 57, 60, 61, 91, 100, 110, 123-4, 128, 131, 140, 153, 155, 156-7
Marylebone Cricket Club 10
Metro-Cammel Carriage & Wagon Company 29
Metropolitan & District Railway 9
Metropolitan Estates Committee 9
Metropolitan & Great Central Joint Committee 140
Metropolitan & LNER Joint 48
Metropolitan Railway 8-10, 30, 40-1, 43, 68, 103, 140

159

THE CHILTERN LINE

Midland Railway 8, 9, 11, 14, 24, 35
Middlesex 11
Middleton Stoney
Mile End Methodist Model Railway Club 127
Milton 55
Milton Keynes 156
Ministry of Food 26
Modernisation Plan (1955) 27
Monks Risborough 134
Montgomery, Sir Bernard 32
Moor Park 32
Moorgate 46
Morris Motor Car 130
'Mosquito' (aeroplane) 70
Motorway 1 27
M40 95, 108, 125
Murder on the Orient Express 124
National Carriers 33
Railway Executive Committee 23
Nazis 25
Neasden 16, 29, 30-1, 38, 40-2, 44, 51, 53, 155
Nettlebed 70
Network Cards 155
Network SouthEast 6, 33-4, 57, 91, 154-5
Newton Longville 130
Night Mail 64
Northampton 111
Northamptonshire 11
North Eastern Region 28
Northern Rubber Special 41
Northolt 17, 19, 31, 40, 44, 53
Northolt Junction 19, 53
Northolt Park 32, 53
Nutt & Sons 19, 98, 100
Nottingham 9, 10, 29, 129
Nottingham (Arkwright Street) 31
Nottinghamshire 10, 11. 14
Nottingham Victoria 4, 29, 31
Old Oak Common 19
Origins of a Modern Myth 10
Orkneys 155
Oxford 5-6, 16-7, 25-6, 31, 38, 54, 59, 70, 75, 78, 81, 107, 110-2, 114-5, 118, 128-30, 140, 143, 149, 150, 153, 156
Oxford Publishing Co 154
Oxfordshire 70, 104
Oxford & Aylesbury Railway 75
Oxford to Cambridge Railway 156
Oxford Canal 108, 114
Oxford Clay 130
Oxford Parkway 156
Oxford University Railway Society 5, 95
Paddington 6, 17, 26, 29, 31-4, 36, 54-5, 59, 66, 74, 79, 97, 105, 117, 118, 120
Paris 10
Parker, F, & Sons Limited 67
Parker, Sir Peter 33
'Parliamentary' 129
Pauling & Co., R W 19
Paxmans 71
Pegler, Alan 118
Peterborough 130
Piccadilly Line 68
Pierce, Jim 70
Pinner Lane 43
Pollitt, William 36
Portman Market 10, 36
Princes Risborough 6. 17, 19, 20, 31, 35, 40, 64, 66, 72, 75-80, 96, 98, 102, 104, 109, 115, 117, 120, 123, 140, 142-6, 149, 150, 155, 156
Quainton 71
Quainton Railway Society 71
Quainton Road 5, 10, 26, 104, 126, 129, 133, 140
Railways Act 1921 24
Railway Executive 28
Rail Users Consultative Committee 33
Reading 17, 25, 123, 149
Regional Railways Board 30
Reid, Bob 154
Retford 41
Rewley Road 26
Rickmansworth 17, 32, 40
Ridgmont 130
Rolt, L T C 13, 108
Romford 26
Rossmore Road 37
Rothschild 67
Rugby 31
Rugby Central 31
Rugby League Cup Final 44
Ruislip Gardens 40
Sandy 26
Saunderton 19, 72-4
Scotland 123, 154
Scott & Middleton 21, 75
'ScotRail' 154
Scottish Region 28
Seer Green 59, 63
'Shakespeare' 114
Seer Green & Jordans 63
Sheffield 14, 29, 31, 61
Sheffield Victoria 53
Shooter, Adrian 155
Souldern 107, 119
South Aylesbury Halt 138
Southcourt 138
South Harrow & Roxeth 53
Southern Railway 24-6, 42
Southern Region 28, 56, 118
South Ruislip 53
South Wales 14
South Yorkshireman 29
Spring Gardens 70
Staines 26
Steeple Claydon 129, 131
Stratford-upon-Avon 34, 124
Stephenson, George 6
Stewartby 130
Stoke Mandeville 138
St Johns Wood Railway 8, 9
St Marylebone Society 33
St Pancras 8, 35
South Eastern Railway 10
South Ruislip 53
South Ruislip & Northolt Junction
St Pancras 35
Sudbury 43
Sudbury & Harrow Road 32, 51, 52
Sudbury Hill 32, 51, 52
Suffragette 72
Swiss Cottage 9
Transport Holding Company 30
Temple, Earl 126
Tesco 59
Thame 16, 18, 31, 76, 78, 80, 143, 148-50
Thames & Chiltern Sub Sector 155
Thames Valley 8
The Aylesbury Railway 139
The Beatles 36
The Department of the Environment 32
British Empire Exhibition 47
The Ipcress File 36
The Stars Look Down 55
The Master Cutler 29, 43, 51, 53, 61, 63
The Network SouthEast Story 154
'The Never Stop Railway' 46, 48-9, 50
'The Phoenix Trail' 149
'The Regency' 32
The Reshaping of British Railways 30
The Shakespeare Limited
'The Victoria' 32
Thorpe House 59
Tollman 36
Totteridge Road 70
Trafford Park 41
Transport Act (1962) 39
Transport User Consultative Committee 32, 68
Travel Cards 155
Travelling Post Office (TPO) 148
Tubbs Lane 110
Twilight of British Rail? 28
Tyseley 93, 142
Utility 70, 71
Uxbridge 68
Uxbridge High Street 55, 62
Vale of Aylesbury 104
Victoria Coach Station 33
Victoria Station 36
Vincent, Mike 154
Wade, Jethro Thomas 71
Walter-Thomson, J 154
Waterloo 36, 94
Water Eaton 6
Watkin, MP, Sir Edward 8-10, 14, 31, 43-4
Watkin's Tower 45
Watlington 17, 94, 142-3, 146-8
Watson, Richard 36
Webster & Cannon 19, 126
Wembley 10, 44, 53
Wembley Carriage Depot 44, 155
Wembley Complex 32, 44
Wembley Hill 43, 45
Wembley History Society 89
Wembley Park 43, 48
Wembley Stadium 47
Westcott 128
West Hampstead 36
Western Region 28, 32, 55
Westminster 19
West Ruislip 30, 45, 52, 54
West Wycombe 19, 67-9, 77
Wheatley 76
Whiteleaf Cross 143
Whiteleaf Halt 134
Widened Lines 46
Willesden 53
Windsor 41
Windsor Chair 70
Wolverhampton 29, 97, 105, 124
Woodhead Tunnel 14
Woodhouse 31
Woodford Halse 23, 30-1, 122-4, 152
Wood Siding 104
World War 1 24, 38, 41, 70, 142, 152
World War 2 24-5, 48, 70, 123
Wotton 13, 97, 126
Wotton Pillinge 130
Wotton Tramway 104, 127
Wotton Underwood 126
Worcester 26
Wroxton Ironstone Co 124
Wycombe Corporation 67
Wycombe Railway 16, 18-9, 21, 66, 75-6, 143, 149
York 31, 123, 151
Yorkshire 9, 14
Zeppelin 25